Fitness Training for Soccer

by Ken Sherry and
Anthony John Harris

REEDSWAIN

**Library of Congress
Cataloging - in - Publication Data**

by Ken Sherry and Anthony John Harris
    Fitness Training for Soccer

ISBN No. 1-59164-035-0
Lib. of Congress Catalog No. 2002094143
© 2002

Editing
Bryan R. Beaver

Front Cover Photo by
EMPICS Ltd.

Printed by
DATA REPRODUCTIONS
Auburn, Michigan

Reedswain Publishing
612 Pughtown Road
Spring City, PA 19475
800.331.5191
www.reedswain.com
info@reedswain.com

Table of Contents

Circuit Training Exercises

Conditioning Games

Goalkeeping Fitness Training Sessions

Defender Fitness Training Sessions

Midfielder Fitness Training Sessions

Attacking Fitness Training Sessions

General Introductions

I have known Tony Harris for several years, and the idea of collaborating on a fitness book only developed into reality after he had read and used a copy of my first book "Soccer Practice Plans for Effective Training".

To put this into practice was not as easy as we had first thought it would be, as Tony lives on the Isle of Wight, UK and I live in Switzerland. However, we finally managed to put ideas to paper and this book is the result.

I hope that it will be of use to all of you coaches who feel that the fitness of players is in the coach's best interest.

Kenneth J. Sherry

As a Royal Marines Commando I was introduced to a varied regime of fitness training. This was designed to ensure that I was ready both mentally and physically to undertake any task put before me.

This high level of fitness also helped when playing soccer. However, when I completed the FA Diploma in the Treatment of Injuries course, I became more aware of the need for positional/functional drills when designing fitness training activities for soccer.

I started to experiment, combining my experience of fitness training with my understanding of soccer to produce player specific training drills, circuit training sessions, running activities and conditioning games. At this point, I approached Ken, after reading his first book, and we decided to combine our skills to produce this book.

All the exercises and drills in this book have been tested for viability by Ken and myself.

I enjoyed collaborating in writing this book and participating in the activities contained within it. I hope you enjoy this book too and that it serves you well in the development of your players.

Anthony John Harris

About this book

This book is specifically designed for soccer coaches and those responsible for the development of players at grass roots level, who perform their training with the minimum amount of equipment.

Fitness training is an essential component of soccer development. The stronger, faster, more agile and balanced the players are combined with a good endurance level, the more you will gain from players in training and in game situations.

Every session should be preceded by a warm up and it is advisable to have a selection of routines to keep players interested. If you are unsure of how to conduct a warm up it is essential that you either attend a fitness course, coaching course or refer to "Soccer Practice Plans for Effective Training".

The fitness training sessions are subdivided into the following sections:

General Fitness Training
Fitness Training Sessions
Circuit Training Sessions
Circuit Training Exercises
Conditioning Games

Positional and Functional Drills
Goalkeeper Fitness Training
Defender Fitness Training
Midfielder Fitness Training
Attacker Fitness Training

All sections have the dimensions and equipment for each activity included. Distances are specified in yards and where possible the relevant field markings have been utilized.

The drills are easy to set up and understand and can be adapted to suit the needs of the player and the aims of the coach in developing fitness, testing fitness and assessing fitness.

Positional and Functional Drills

The positional and functional drills have been designed to be used as a functional fitness assessment of players. The coach can measure the players' performance against previous tests to measure their ongoing fitness. In drills where a ball is included the outcome of the contact with the ball is not important. The ball is included simply to provide realism in the players' movements.

The drills are designed to reproduce possible actions and movements experienced in a game, dependant upon the actual playing position. Of course, many are generic to soccer as a whole but each playing position has a specific role to play within the team and players must be prepared to carry out this role for the duration of a game.

The key to this has to be realism in training and if players are introduced to training that reflects their role at a high intensity level and they are tested and measured regularly, then they will be prepared to undertake the role of that position. Combine this training with specific coaching and other sport related education and the preparation is complete.

Left Side of Page

Fitness Aims

This outlines the fitness aims for the session.

Layout Description

This describes the specific area of the field needed to be set up for the activity and explains how to position equipment such as cones and balls.

Organization

This provides an overview of how to conduct the session and to achieve the fitness aims.

System of measurement

When using the activity to assess and measure fitness, the activity must be measurable and reproducible. This section describes how to measure a player's performance and reproduce the same action to achieve an accurate assessment every time the drill is performed.

Right Side of Page

Fitness Record

This space allows the user to record the outcome of the session and the performance statistics for each player. Factors such as repetitions completed and measurement of time can be recorded. This can be filed for future use to compare player fitness progression or even assess fitness of players after injury.

This page could be photocopied and a fitness record file produced for every player. This can be kept at the club or by the player and will provide an excellent overview of progression or regression of the players' fitness. It will also provide the coach with evidence to support player selection and the development of training activities.

Session comments and variations

This provides comments, suggestions and variations on the selected session. All the sessions can be adapted to suit the needs of the coach and the age and fitness of the players. The performance statistics of the variations should also be recorded in the players' fitness records.

Soccer Fitness Training

A soccer fitness-training program introduces a player to a gradual escalation of difficulty in physical training, a process that allows the body to adjust to the ever-greater needs of the soccer player.

The heart becomes stronger and the muscles become firmer in response to fitness training.

The stronger the heart becomes, the more the body is able to respond and therefore the stronger the muscles become.

By reducing the fat content of the body, this will help the heart and lungs to work more efficiently and easily because there is less resistance to the blood and oxygen flow within the body.

Components of Fitness

This can be remembered using the five 'S' s.
Suppleness - flexibility
Strength - power
Speed - and agility
Stamina - cardiovascular respiratory endurance
Skill - techniques of game performance under pressure.

Each component is relevant to soccer although some have more importance than others.

Fitness Components	Important	Very Important
Cardiovascular Respiratory Fitness		X
Muscular Endurance		X
Strength	X	
Power		X
Speed and Agility		X
Flexibility		X
Skill		X

Fitness Factors

Frequency:
The number of fitness training sessions over a given period of time (one week). A minimum of three sessions per week is recommended to develop significant increases in fitness levels.

Intensity:
Intensity is how hard a player trains. This is individual and players may work at different levels and for varying lengths of time.
Intensity will directly effect the effectiveness of the training. Too little intensity will not achieve a training gain, but too much may lead to injury and over training.

Overload:
Training should be progressive and structured to produce an increasing overload on the body. As the body adapts so the training load can be increased.

Time:
This simply refers to the time spent training in a session. This will vary but should reflect the timeframes within the sport.

Type of Exercise:
Sessions will vary to achieve the aim of the player/coach and different types of exercise (aerobic running, anaerobic sprints, circuits etc.) may be employed.

F.I.T.T. (Frequency - Intensity - Time - Type of Exercise):
These four factors form the FITT principle for soccer fitness training routines.

Specificity:
The aim of the sessions should be to improve players as soccer players, not produce sprinters etc. Therefore, sessions must relate to the demands of the sport.

Reversibility:
'Use it' or 'lose it'. Unless you continue to train your fitness levels will decline. This is individual and some people can maintain fitness longer, but the decline will still be evident.

Fitness Training Sessions General

First of all we must consider that a soccer player will have several different phases of activity during a game such as standing, walking, jogging, running at controlled pace and sprinting.

The first 2, standing and walking, we all know do not need to be trained, as players are generally very apt in these qualities.
The third activity, jogging, is normally trained in warming up, warming down and general activity around the training field. This should not be avoided, however, because some form of running at one speed for a distance is very essential.

The last 2, running at a controlled pace and sprinting, should be trained in special sessions and whenever possible should include the ball.

There should always be a balance between running and recovery to achieve the required fitness.

The number of repetitions can be increased and the recovery time shortened, as the players become more fit.

Practice recommendations
for general fitness training sessions

All these fitness sessions allow for continuous movement with and without the ball.
This type of training can be varied in repetitions and recovery time.
Always build up the sessions over several weeks with increased repetitions and shorter recovery times.
To increase the fitness, the number of players to a grid should be decreased and the recovery time reduced accordingly.
The fitness can also be improved by increasing the number of times each player performs the activity.
To make it more interesting, allow players and teams to compete against each other.

Fitness Training Sessions

1. Shuttle sprinting and dribbling
2. Power hopping
3. Running with the ball around the cones
4. Cross shuttle running
5. Standing forward jump
6. Recovery runs
7. The M run
8. The figure of 8 run
9. Shuttle sprinting and collect the ball
10. Pass and create space

Equipment needed for the Training Sessions:

⊙ A set of cones for marking the training area.

⊙ A long tape measure for setting the distances for the training layout.

⊙ A stop watch for evaluating the fitness of the players.

⊙ At least one ball between two players.

⊙ First aid bag in case of injuries.

Shuttle sprinting and dribbling

Fitness Aims: Sprinting and dribbling at controlled speed

To train players to sprint and dribble with the ball at controlled speed.
Recover while 3 other players perform the task.

Layout Description:

Set out a grid of 9 cones 5 yards apart in one line.

Set out enough grids to accommodate the whole team.

Use 4 only players for each grid.

Have a minimum of 2 players each side of the grid.

One ball should be placed at one side of the grid.

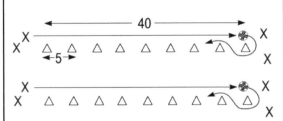

Organization:

The first player sprints to collect a ball from the other side of the grid and dribbles it back through the cones at a controlled speed. The next player runs from the opposite side to collect the ball and the practice alternates. The repetitions are dependent on the age of the players and general fitness but each player should run at least 5 times.

Fitness Record

Date:
Number of players to each grid:
Number of repetitions:
Time of team a: b: c: d:

Date:
Number of players to each grid:
Number of repetitions:
Time of team a: b: c: d:

Date:
Number of players to each grid:
Number of repetitions:
Time of team a: b: c: d:

Date:
Number of players to each grid:
Number of repetitions:
Time of team a: b: c: d:

Training Variations:

To make the drill more interesting have the teams compete against each other.

This drill can be used so that players will dribble in both directions. This means that the team would be on one side of the grid and dribble to the end and back.

Power hopping

Fitness Aims: **Improve leg power**

To develop leg strength by power hopping on 1 leg to obtain the greatest distance.
Recover while other players perform the task.

Layout Description:

Set out grids 5 yards by 9 yards using at least 8 cones.

Use 2 separate cones for each player to mark the distance for the left and right hopping leg.

Use a maximum of 4 players for each grid.

Where possible use players with the same ability in one grid.

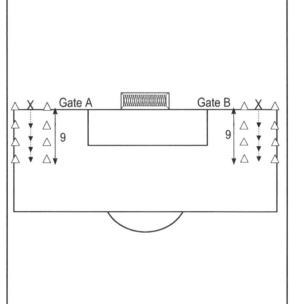

Organization:

The player must stand with feet behind the line. On the command 'GO' the player hops 4 times on 1 leg as far as possible, and then repeats using the other leg. The players should alternate using the right and the left leg. Mark the greatest distance achieved for each leg.

Fitness Record

Date: Player:
Right leg greatest distance:
Left leg greatest distance:

Date: Player:
Right leg greatest distance:
Left leg greatest distance:

Date: Player:
Right leg greatest distance:
Left leg greatest distance:

Date: Player:
Right leg greatest distance:
Left leg greatest distance:

Date: Player:
Right leg greatest distance:
Left leg greatest distance:

Date: Player:
Right leg greatest distance:
Left leg greatest distance:

Date: Player:
Right leg greatest distance:
Left leg greatest distance:

Training Variations:

For strength fitness the players should hop in 1 direction with 4 hops and back with 4 hops using the opposite leg. This can be a repetition drill where each player hops 3 times through the grid. Check that the hopping distance does not become too short.
For longer hopping distances allow a 5-yard run up to the gate.

Running with the ball around the cones

Fitness Aims:	**Sprint and controlled running with the ball**

To train players to sprint and dribble with the ball at controlled speed.
Recover while a minimum of 3 other players perform the task

Layout Description:

Set out a grid 10 X 25 yards with 12 cones in 2 lines of 6 cones. Make the distance between the cones 5 yards.

Set out enough grids to accommodate the whole team.

Use a maximum of 4 players for each grid.

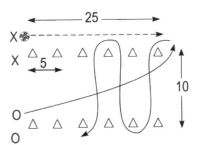

Organization:

The player starts by sprinting diagonally across the grid to collect the ball that is passed by another player. The player runs with the ball at controlled speed, through the cones until reaching the end of the grid.
Players take turns to complete the run but repetitions depend on the age of the players and their general fitness, although each player should complete the task at least 5 times.

Fitness Record			
Date:	Repetitions:		
Team Times a:	b:	c:	d:
Date:	Repetitions:		
Team Times a:	b:	c:	d:
Date:	Repetitions:		
Team Times a:	b:	c:	d:
Date:	Repetitions:		
Team Times a:	b:	c:	d:
Date:	Repetitions:		
Team Times a:	b:	c:	d:
Date:	Repetitions:		
Team Times a:	b:	c:	d:
Date:	Repetitions:		
Team Times a:	b:	c:	d:

Training Variations:

This drill can be competitive with the teams starting at the same time and checking to see who wins. Make sure that the drill is correctly carried out, otherwise the player must start again.

This drill can be used with 2 players starting at the same time from either side of the grid. When the players dribble back through the cones they can attempt to disrupt the other player by attempting to kick the ball away.

Cross shuttle running

Fitness Aims: **Sprinting and passing**

To train players to sprint diagonally and pass the ball with speed and accuracy.
Quick recovery while the other player plays the ball.

Layout Description:

Set out a grid 10 X 10 yards using cones to mark each corner.

Set out enough grids to accommodate the whole team.

Use a maximum of 8 players for each grid.

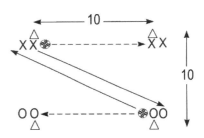

Organization:

The first player passes the ball directly across the grid then sprints diagonally across to the other side of the grid. The next player controls the ball and passes the ball back along the grid, and sprints diagonally across to the other side of the grid. If the players keep losing the ball or the running pattern becomes confusing, start again but at a slower pace. Allocate a time and check how many completed diagonal runs for each team.

Fitness Record

Date: Time Allocation:
Number of runs for each team:
a: b: c: d: e: f:

Date: Time Allocation:
Number of runs for each team:
a: b: c: d: e: f:

Date: Time Allocation:
Number of runs for each team:
a: b: c: d: e: f:

Date: Time Allocation:
Number of runs for each team:
a: b: c: d: e: f:

Date: Time Allocation:
Number of runs for each team:
a: b: c: d: e: f:

Date: Time Allocation:
Number of runs for each team:
a: b: c: d: e: f:

Training Variations:

For a fitter team you can use only 4 players or as a progression, start with 8 players and establish the 4 player version as a goal.

This drill can be competitive with the teams starting at the same time and checking to see who wins. Make sure that the drill is correctly carried out, otherwise the player must start again.

Standing forward jump

Fitness Aims:	Improve leg power

To develop leg strength by power jumping using both legs to obtain the greatest distance.
Recover while other players perform the task.
speed and accuracy.

Layout Description:

Set out grids 5 yards across by 6 yards using at least 6 cones.

Use a separate cone for each player to mark the greatest distance for each jump.

Use a maximum of 4 players to each grid.

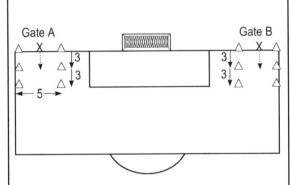

Organization:

The player must stand with feet behind the line. On the command 'GO' the player jumps as far as possible to obtain the greatest distance.

The player may use the whole body movement to obtain the greatest distance without moving the feet before jumping. Mark the greatest distance obtained by each player.

Fitness Record

Date	Player	Distance:
Date	Player	Distance:
Date	Player	Distance:
Date	Player	Distance:
Date	Player	Distance:
Date	Player	Distance:
Date	Player	Distance:
Date	Player	Distance:
Date	Player	Distance:
Date	Player	Distance:

Training Variations:

For strength fitness the players can also jump backward after the forward jump. Record both the backward and the forward jump.

This can be a repetition drill where each player jumps 3 times through the grid both forward and backward. Check that the jumping distances do not become too short.

Recovery runs

Fitness Aims: **Sprinting, passing and recovery**

To train players to sprint and pass the ball with speed and accuracy.
Recover after an opposing player with the ball.

Layout Description:

Set out a grid 10 X 30 yards with 2 passing zones of 5 yards either side of the grid.

Set out enough grids to accommodate the whole team.

Use a maximum of 6 players for each grid.

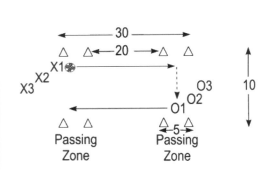

Organization:

The X1 player starts with the ball in the 5 yard passing zone and runs the 20 yard zone with the ball to the opposite 5 yard passing zone and passes to the next player O1. O1 controls the ball and runs in the opposite direction to the other passing zone and passes the ball to X2. When O1 has controlled the ball X1 runs back after O1 to the X1 starting zone. This is repeated with O1 chasing after X2.

Fitness Record

Date: Time Element:
Number of repetitions for each team:
A: B: C: D:

Date: Time Element:
Number of repetitions for each team:
A: B: C: D:

Date: Time Element:
Number of repetitions for each team:
A: B: C: D:

Date: Time Element:
Number of repetitions for each team:
A: B: C: D:

Date: Time Element:
Number of repetitions for each team:
A: B: C: D:

Date: Time Element:
Number of repetitions for each team:
A: B: C: D:

Training Variations:

Count the number of repetitions for each team for a given time, so that the teams can compete against each other.

After running with the ball to the opposite passing zone and passing to the next player, the player stays in the zone waiting for the next pass. In this case, use only 4 players to a grid.

The M run

Fitness Aims:	**Speed and endurance**

This session should develop speed and agility.

Layout Description:	

Set out a grid 10 X 20 yards with 1 cone in the middle to create an "M" shape.

Set out enough grids to accommodate the whole team.

Use a maximum of 4 players for each grid.

Place a ball at cone B.

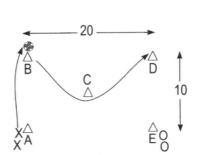

Organization:

The player starts at cone (A), sprints to cone (B), picks up the ball and sprints around cone (C) then leaves the ball at cone (D). The player then sprints to cone (E) to tag the next player who repeats the run in the opposite direction. Make sure that the balls are positioned at the correct cones after the ball has been carried.

Fitness Record

Date: Time Element:
Number of player runs:
Team: A: B: C: D: E:

Date: Time Element:
Number of player runs:
Team: A: B: C: D: E:

Date: Time Element:
Number of player runs:
Team: A: B: C: D: E:

Date: Time Element:
Number of player runs:
Team: A: B: C: D: E:

Date: Time Element:
Number of player runs:
Team: A: B: C: D: E:

Date: Time Element:
Number of player runs:
Team: A: B: C: D: E:

Training Variations:

Teams should compete against each other for a set time period to make the players work harder.

Instead of picking the ball up the player can dribble from cone (B) to cone (D) and leave the ball for the next player coming in the opposite direction.

The figure 8 run

Fitness Aims: **Endurance and recovery**

To train players to run and change direction using an interval based running activity.
This session should develop endurance and recovery rate.

Layout Description:

Set out a grid 10 X 30 yards with 6 cones creating a figure eight.

Set out enough grids to accommodate the whole team.

Use only 6 players for each grid.

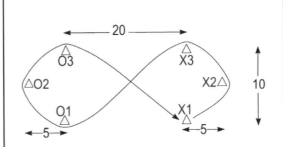

Organization:

Each player must stand on one cone in the figure eight. On the command 'GO' all the X players run around the figure eight and end up back at their starting cone. As soon as all X players have completed a circuit and are back on station at their own start cone, the O players can start running.

This is repeated for a given time period. Check which team wins each time but set the number of repetitions depending on the age and or fitness of the players.
A sequence is when all players have completed the run.

Fitness Record

Date:
Time of each sequence:
Team A: B: C: D: E:

Date:
Time of each sequence:
Team A: B: C: D: E:

Date:
Time of each sequence:
Team A: B: C: D: E:

Date:
Time of each sequence:
Team A: B: C: D: E:

Date:
Time of each sequence:
Team A: B: C: D: E:

Training Variations:

The X players run around the figure eight with the ball and end up back at their starting cone. As soon as all X players have completed a circuit and are back on station at their own start cone, the O players can start running with the ball.
The players must run around the outside of the cones and the O players cannot start until all the X players have returned to their cone with the ball.
If there are not enough players for 6 to a grid use a balanced number i.e. 15 players: 3 X players and 2 O players to a grid.

Shuttle sprinting and collect the ball

Fitness Aims: Sprinting and changing direction

To train players to sprint and change direction.
This session should develop speed and agility.

Layout Description:

Set out a grid 10 X 20 yards with cones in 2 lines. The distance between the cones should be 5 yards.

Place a ball for each player at the opposite side of the grid.

Set out enough grids to accommodate the whole team.

Use a maximum of 8 players for each grid divided into 2 teams.

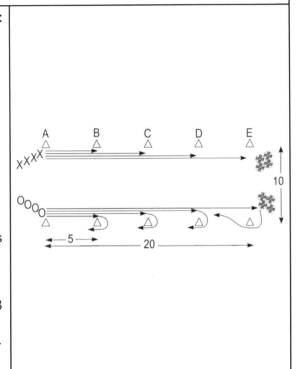

Organization:

The player must stand with feet behind cone (A). On the command 'GO' the player runs to cone (B) and returns to cone (A). The player then runs to cone (C) and so on, returning each time to the start cone (A). On the last run to cone (E) the player should collect a ball and dribble back through the cones to the start cone (A) and tag the next player to repeat the same sequence. When the last X and O have finished the sequence is complete. Determine who wins each time but set the number of repetitions depending on the age and or fitness of the players.

Fitness Record

Date:
Team Players:

O1	O2
O3	O4
X1	X2
X3	X4
Time Team O:	Time Team X:

Date:
Team Players:

O1	O2
O3	O4
X1	X2
X3	X4
Time Team O:	Time Team X:

Date:
Team Players:

O1	O2
O3	O4
X1	X2
X3	X4
Time Team O:	Time Team X:

Training Variations:

The drill can be used so that the player starts with the ball at cone (A) and runs to each cone with the ball and ends up leaving the ball at the other end and sprinting back.
The next player sprints to collect the ball from the other end and runs with the ball in the reverse direction ending up giving the ball to the next player.

Pass and create space

Fitness Aims: **Passing and sprinting to create space**

To train players to pass the ball and sprint in the opposite direction to create space.
This session should develop speed, endurance and agility.

Layout Description:

Set out a grid 20 X 20 yards using at least 16 cones 5 yards apart in a square.

Place a ball on each side of the grid at cones (A and B).

Set out enough grids to accommodate the whole team.

Use a maximum of 6 players for each grid.

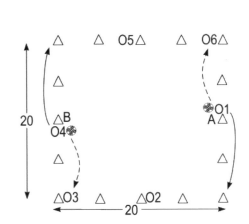

Organization:
Start with the players (O1) and (O4) opposite each other in the middle of the grid. Both players start with a ball and on the command 'GO' the player passes the ball to the next player counter-clockwise and runs clockwise in the opposite direction to the next cone. (O1) passes to (O6) and (O4) passes to (O3). Both balls should be passed around the square in the same direction and players should move in the opposite direction.
Set a time limit for the practice depending on the age and or fitness of the players. Start with a 2 minute time allocation and increase as fitness allows.

Fitness Record

Date: Time Allocation:
Team Players:
O1   O2
O3   O4
O5   O6
How far did the ball go for the allocated time
Ball A: Ball B:

Date: Time Allocation:
Team Players:
O1   O2
O3   O4
O5   O6
How far did the ball go for the allocated time
Ball A: Ball B:

Date: Time Allocation:
Team Players:
O1   O2
O3   O4
O5   O6
How far did the ball go for the allocated time
Ball A: Ball B:

Training Variations:

For a fitness drill add 2 more players to the vacant corner cones and use 2 more balls. This can be complicated so start off slowly with 2 balls so the players can find a rhythm and add the 2 extra balls when the passing is good. The passing must be quick and accurate, otherwise the balls will always be out of play.

Circuit Training Sessions General

Circuit training is a proven method of improving muscular endurance and can be adapted to produce positive fitness gains in general fitness, muscular strength and speed.

Circuit training will produce all-round fitness and can be undertaken almost anywhere. All you need is knowledge of the exercises and some variations, which can be adapted to the area where you intend to train.

In extreme cases, it is only necessary to use one and half times the body length as an area to train in and still be effective, but any open space outdoors or in a hall is ideal.

The aim of circuit training is the progressive development of cardiovascular fitness and the muscular system to achieve all-round fitness.

Circuit training can be enjoyable and can be performed in groups or as an individual.

Individuals can work at their own pace and the circuit can be adapted to suit all levels of fitness within the group.

Equipment needed Circuit Training:

- An area to train can be any open space, preferably out doors or in a hall.

- A stop watch when evaluating the fitness of the players.

- First Aid Bag in case of injuries.

- Cones and balls.

Circuit Training Sessions

1. Threes up circuit
2. Ton ups
3. The star circuit
4. Sprint circuits
5. Black jack circuit
6. The two minute killer
7. Pairs skill circuit
8. Four corners
9. The accumulator
10. The big one

Types of Circuit Training

- Timed Circuit.
- Individual Circuit.
- Repetition Circuit.
- Running Circuit.

The circuits included are all variations of these four methods.

Soccer requires a blend of aerobic and anaerobic fitness, therefore circuits should include activities to develop both, as well as balance, coordination and general muscular endurance.

Threes up Circuit

Circuit Aims:

A group of 3 players should work together to perform eight different MAT exercises.

The shuttle running with the ball determines the timing.

Circuit Exercises

1: Shuttle running: running with the ball to each cone in order and returning to the start cone. On the last cone the player passes back along the line of cones to the next player coming from station 2 and moves to station 3.

2: Mat exercise sequence:

a. Press Up.

b. Half Squats.

c. Back Extension.

d. Crunches.

e. Squat Thrust.

f. Triceps Dips.

g. Side Bends.

h. Crunches with a Twist.

3: Ground passes against the bench.

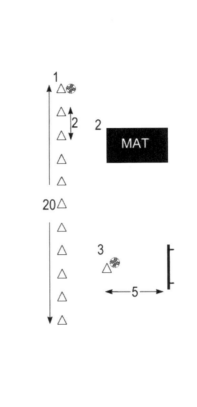

Circuit Sequence:

Create groups of 3 players who work together going through the circuit. The group moves around the circuit changing the MAT exercise each time. The circuit timing is determined by the shuttle running exercise. When this is finished the player on station 3 moves to 2 and 2 moves to 1 and station 1 (the shuttle running player) goes to station 3.

Fitness Record

Date:
Player Names:
1.
2.
3.

Number of exercies achived:
Press up -
Squats -
Back extension -
Crunches -
Squat thrust -
Triceps dips -
Side bends -
Crunches with a twist -

Total time for the circuit:

Circuit Variations and Comments:

The players on exercises 2 and 3 must continue until the player on the shuttle exercise is in position to pass the ball to the next shuttle player who is on the mat exercises.

The players move as quickly as possible to the next station, as this will have an impact on the total time of the circuit.

A ball can be used for certain mat exercises where possible i.e. squats where the player holds the ball out in front.

Different variations can be used on the shuttle run e.g. the player runs around the cones or runs backward dragging the ball with one foot around the cones alternating the foot on the ball.

Ton ups

Circuit Aims:

Players should aim to complete 100 repetitions of each exercise and a nominated running distance completed by performing shuttle runs

Circuit Exercises

1: Press Ups
2: Crunches
3: Squat Thrust
4: Back Extension
5: Triceps Dips
6: Half Sit Ups
7: Bench Jumps
8: Side Bends

Sprint 20 Yards

```
4                           5
   MAT              BOX

                    BOX
3                           6
  △    △              MAT

2                           7

   MAT

1                           8

   MAT             △    △

 △                          △
 ←——————— 20 ———————→
```

Circuit Sequence:

Players may perform exercises in any order and any amount of repetitions as long as they complete 100 repetitions of each exercise and the required distance for the shuttle run. For each station make enough room so that at least 2 players can exercise at the same time. This will allow at least 8 players on the circuit at 1 time.

Fitness Record

Date:

Player Names:

1.   Total time:

         Number of shuttle runs:

2.   Total time:

         Number of shuttle runs:

3.   Total time:

         Number of shuttle runs:

4.   Total time:

         Number of shuttle runs:

5.   Total time:

         Number of shuttle runs:

6.   Total time:

         Number of shuttle runs:

7.   Total time:

         Number of shuttle runs:

8.   Total time:

         Number of shuttle runs:

Circuit Variations and Comments:

Have 2 players work together first. The players must make the same number of repetitions for each exercise.

The players may have difficulty remembering how many exercises have been achieved, so set a specific number for each exercise and the number of rotations of the circuit.

For younger players and players who are not fit, start with 30 to 40 repetitions and work up to the 100 repetitions for each exercise over a period of time.

The star circuit

Circuit Aims:
Players exercise at each station for 15 seconds.
After each exercise the players run to the center and onto the next exercise moving clockwise around the circuit.

Circuit Exercises

1: Bench Jump
2: Triceps Dips
3: Half Sit Ups
4: Step Ups
5: Press Ups
6: Crunches
7: Half Squats
8: Arm Punching
9: Side Bends
10: Crunches with Twist

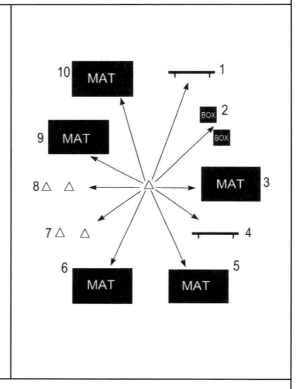

Circuit Sequence:

Use up to 10 players on each circuit starting on a separate exercise. The players make 3 circuits with 15 seconds for each exercise. The players must run to the middle of the star and stop for an interval before running on to the next exercise. Time the exercises for 15 seconds and use commands such as 'GO' and 'STOP' or a whistle. The interval time between exercises will depend on how fit the players are. The interval time can be decreased as the players become fitter.

Fitness Record
Player Name: Date:
1.   Time on each exercise: Interval time:
2.   Time on each exercise: Interval time:
3.   Time on each exercise: Interval time:
4.   Time on each exercise: Interval time:
5.   Time on each exercise: Interval time:
6.   Time on each exercise: Interval time:
7.   Time on each exercise: Interval time:
8.   Time on each exercise: Interval time:
9.   Time on each exercise: Interval time:
10.   Time on each exercise: Interval time:

Circuit Variations and Comments:

Have players work in pairs which will increase the work at each exercise.
Vary the running to and from the middle of the star by having the players run forwards to the station and backwards to the middle of the star.

The 15 seconds per exercise can be varied depending on the age and fitness of the players.
The optimum is to increase the time at each exercise and decrease the interval between exercises.

Sprint circuits

Circuit Aims:

Each of the eight exercises should be performed for 20 seconds with a sprint between exercises.
The players perform the circuit one after another until all have finished.

Circuit Exercises

1: Half Squats
2: Press Ups
3: Crunches
4: Back Extension
5: Alternate leg Squat Thrust
6: Arm Punching
7: Side Bends
8: Tuck Jump

40 yard run back to the finish

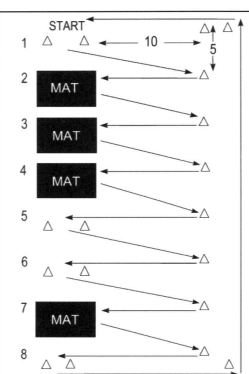

Circuit Sequence:

The players start one after another in sequence. The exercises should be performed for 20 seconds and on completion the player should sprint to the cone and on to the next station. Time the exercises for 20 seconds and use commands such as 'GO' and 'STOP' or a whistle. When the players complete the exercise at station 8 they run back to the finish and continue around the circuit. The number of circuits will depend on the age and the fitness of the players.

Fitness Record
Player Name: Date:
1.   Time on each exercise:
Number of circuits:
2.   Time on each exercise:
Number of circuits:
3.   Time on each exercise:
Number of circuits:
4.   Time on each exercise:
Number of circuits:
5.   Time on each exercise:
Number of circuits:
6.   Time on each exercise:
Number of circuits:
7.   Time on each exercise:
Number of circuits:
8.   Time on each exercise:
Number of circuits:

Circuit Variations and Comments:

Between exercises the players can vary the running to and from the cone. This can be rotated between running sideways, running backwards, hopping and skipping.

As a variation have the players work in pairs which will increase the work at each exercise.

Have a timed interval stop on the cones before sprinting to the next exercise.

Black jack circuit

Circuit Aims:

Players perform exercises depending on the face value of the card turned over. Players must guess if the next card is higher or lower than the previous card. If wrong all players perform the required number of sprints and reps for that value, but if correct the coach moves to next player.

Circuit Exercises	
Card value	**Exercise**
2	Crunches
3	Triceps Dips
4	Squat Thrusts
5	Back Extensions
6	Crunch and Twist
7	Arm Punches
8	Alternate leg Squat Thrust
9	Trunk Twist
10/red jack	Press Ups
QKA:	Side Bends

Ten-yard sprints

◄─── 10 ───► ◄─── 10 ───►

△ MAT X▲O △
△ MAT X▲O △
△ MAT X▲O △
△ MAT X▲O △
△ MAT X▲O △
△ MAT X▲O △
△ MAT X▲O △
△ MAT X▲O △

Circuit Sequence:

The players sit back to back in pairs and the coach selects a pair of players. The coach turns over the top card in the pack and 1 player must decide if the next card is higher or lower. If the player is correct, move to the next pair of players, otherwise all players must perform the exercise selected by the face value of the card as follows:

2 to 5	2 sprints 10 reps
6 to 9	2 sprints 15 reps
10/red jack	4 sprints 15 reps
QKA	2 sprints 20 reps
Pair	8 sprints 10 reps
A Black Jack	10 sprints 10 reps

Fitness Record

Player Name: Date: Session Time:

1.
2.
3.
4.
5.
6.
7.
8.
9.
10.
11.
12.
13.
14.
15.
16.

Circuit Variations and Comments:

This session can be worked just in pairs where the first pair calls the card for the next pair and only the next pair performs the exercise accordingly.

Instead of the sprints the players must run around the whole grid and end up at their mat to perform the exercise. This will create confusion if all players run around at the same time so only use this when just one pair at a time performs the exercise.

To keep it simple, use a set number of sprints and repetitions and use the card value to select the exercise.

The two minute killer

Circuit Aims:
This is a very intense exercise sequence intended for fit players only.
The players perform one repetition of four different exercises in sequence for 2 minutes.

Circuit Exercises

1: Half Sit Ups
2: Press Ups
3: Squat Thrust
4: Star Jump

Run Between
Exercises

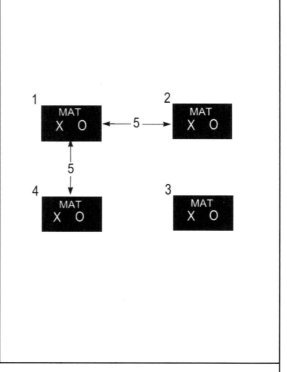

Circuit Sequence:

Players perform one repetition of each exercise in sequence running from one exercise to the next for two minutes. Record the number of completed combinations of exercises in 2 minutes. One combination is one rep of each of the four exercises i.e. 1x Half Sit up, 1 x Press Up, 1 x Squat Thrust, 1x Star Jump.

Set out the circuit so that it is a square and the distance is the same between each mat. The distance should be at least 5 yards between each of the mats.

Fitness Record	
Player Name:	Date:
1.	Number of exercises:
2.	Number of exercises:
3.	Number of exercises:
4.	Number of exercises:
5.	Number of exercises:
6.	Number of exercises:
7.	Number of exercises:
8.	Number of exercises:
9.	Number of exercises:
10.	Number of exercises:
11.	Number of exercises:
12.	Number of exercises:
13.	Number of exercises:
14.	Number of exercises:
15.	Number of exercises:
16.	Number of exercises:

Circuit Variations and Comments:

Have the players work in pairs, which will increase the work at each exercise.

Vary the running around the circuit by having the players run forwards between mats 1 and 2, and 3 and 4 and backwards between mats 2 and 3, and 4 and 1.

This session could be used in conjunction with other training i.e. running, dribbling or ball skill practices.

Pairs skill circuit

Circuit Aims:
Two players do the activities together around the whole field. Most activities require using a ball either individually or as a pair.

Circuit Exercises
1. Ground passing between 2 players.
2. Dribble the ball around the cones three times.
3. Half sit-ups with the ball in the hands.
4. Running with the ball 3 times.
5. Heading the ball to each other.
6. Passing on the move between 2 players 3 times.
7. Press-ups over the ball touching it with the chest.
8. Pass and control the ball between 2 players using the right foot.
9. Side Volley between 2 players
10. Pass and Control the ball between 2 players using the left foot.
11: Alternate leg Squat Thrust

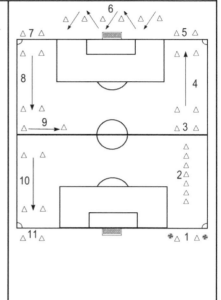

Circuit Sequence:
Use the whole soccer field with players working in pairs. The players have a ball and move around the circuit counter-clockwise, all starting at station 1.

The first players pass the ball to each other 20 times and move on to dribbling through the cones. The pair dribble through the cones once forward and back and forward again. As soon as the pair has completed exercise 1 the next pair can start passing the ball to each other. When the pair at station 2 have finished and moved on to exercise 3 the next pair can dribble through cones and the third pair start with the passing. The next pair arriving at the station controls the timing. As soon as the next pair arrives at the station the pair there must move on to the next exercise.

Fitness Record

Player Name:	Date:
1.	Time around the circuit:
2.	Time around the circuit:
3.	Time around the circuit:
4.	Time around the circuit:
5.	Time around the circuit:
6.	Time around the circuit:
7.	Time around the circuit:
8.	Time around the circuit:
9.	Time around the circuit:
10.	Time around the circuit:
11.	Time around the circuit:
12.	Time around the circuit:
13.	Time around the circuit:
14.	Time around the circuit:
15.	Time around the circuit:
16.	Time around the circuit:

Circuit Variations and Comments:

The timing of exercise 2 and exercise 4, which require the player to either dribble or run with the ball, controls this session.

This session can also be timed with 20 seconds for each exercise and use commands such 'GO' and 'STOP' or a whistle to move to the next exercise.

The players must always take their ball with them after each exercise, even when the exercise does not require or only requires 1 ball.

Four corners

Circuit Aims:
The players do exercises at each corner and perform a running activity in between.

Circuit Exercises	

Circuit Exercises

1: Press Up over the ball
2: Run pushing the ball with the bottom of the right foot.
3: Run pushing the ball with the bottom of the left foot.
4: Half Sit-ups with the ball in the hands.
5: Running back-wards dragging the ball with alternate feet.
6: Squat thrust
7: Run forward with the ball using alter-nate feet
8: Run, juggling the ball in the air
9: Back Extension

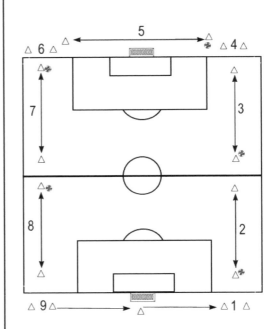

Circuit Sequence:

Use the whole soccer field. Body exercises are performed at each corner of the field (exercises 1,4, 6 and 9).
Time the corner exercises for 20 seconds while the other players perform the running activities between the cones.

Fitness Record

Date: Exercise time: Interval time:

Player Name:

1.   Number of circuits:
2.   Number of circuits:
3.   Number of circuits:
4.   Number of circuits:
5.   Number of circuits:
6.   Number of circuits:
7.   Number of circuits:
8.   Number of circuits:
9.   Number of circuits:
10.   Number of circuits:
11.   Number of circuits:
12.   Number of circuits:
13.   Number of circuits:
14.   Number of circuits:
15.   Number of circuits:
16.   Number of circuits:

Circuit Variations and Comments:

Different exercises can be introduced, especially for the running and working with the ball exercises. The running exercise can be a combination of all 4 suggested exercises where the player does an exercise in one direction and another in the opposite direction.

The players can either run immediately to the next exercise or have an interval of 10 seconds between exercises. This will depend very much on the fitness of the players and the age group of the team. Extend the exercise time and reduce the interval as the players become fitter.

The accumulator

Circuit Aims:
Players work in groups performing exercises the length of the field.
The exercises increase the number of repetitions performed over 3 circuits.

Circuit Exercises

1: Press ups
2: Hop on one foot
3: Hop on the other foot
4: Sit ups
5: Run backwards
6: Sprint
7: Tuck Jump

Jog back to the start

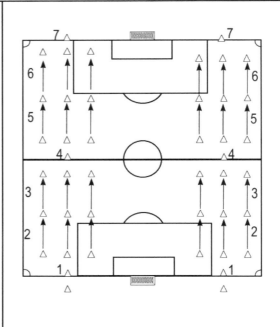

Circuit Sequence:

Create groups of 4 or 6 players. The first group should perform the exercises up to exercise 4 before the next group starts. This will ensure that the groups perform at the same time through circuits.
The players must run as a group and repeat the circuit 3 times, increasing the repetitions for exercises 1, 4 and 7 for each circuit e.g.
Circuit 1   10 repetitions
Circuit 2   15 repetitions
Circuit 3   20 repetitions

Fitness Record

Date:

Group 1   Time for the whole circuit:
Player Names
1.   2.
3.   4.
5.   6.

Group 2   Time for the whole circuit:
Player Names
1.   2.
3.   4.
5.   6.

Group 3   Time for the whole circuit:
Player Names
1.   2.
3.   4.
5.   6.

Circuit Variations and Comments:

Start with 5 repetitions of exercises 1,4 and 7 and build on the number of circuits. The repetitions can be increased to 10, 20, 30 but the players need to be fit for this kind of circuit.

Exercises 2, 3, 5, and 6 can be changed to running with the ball, running backwards with the ball, juggling with the ball and heading the ball while running.

The big one

Circuit Aims:

This circuit can accommodate large numbers of players but can be difficult to control.

Players work in teams of four and move as a team between stations.

Circuit Exercises

1: Run and pass to the next player then go to the back of the line.

2: Run and pass to the next player recover and chase the player with the ball. Start at alternate ends.

3: One player runs to head the ball and recovers, players take turns.

4: Run in front of the goal and perform three jumps touching the cross bar, run back behind the goal while the next player runs in front of the goal.

5: Juggle the ball.

6: Star run.

7: Dribble around the cones and pass to the next player.

8: Shuttle sprints, pick up the ball.

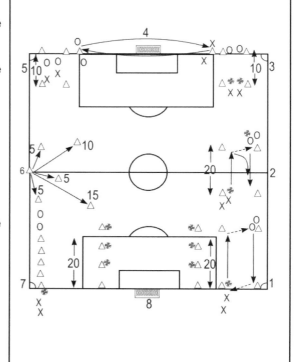

Circuit Sequence:

Create teams of four players who work around the circuit together. Keep a time limit and use a whistle to move on to the next exercise. Use the more demanding exercises as a time guide for the exercise time limit.

Fitness Record

Date:	Exercise time:	Interval time:
Group 1	Player Names	
1.	2.	
3.	4.	
Group 2	Player Names	
1.	2.	
3.	4.	
Group 3	Player Names	
1.	2.	
3.	4.	
Group 4	Player Names	
1.	2.	
3.	4.	
Group 4	Player Names	
1.	2.	
3.	4.	

Circuit Variations and Comments:

This session can also be timed with 20 seconds for each exercise and use commands such 'GO' and 'STOP' or a whistle to move to the next exercise.

The players can either run immediately to the next exercise or have an interval of 10 to 20 seconds between exercises. This will depend very much on the fitness of the players and the age group of the team. Extend the exercise time and reduce the interval as the players become fitter.

The players must leave the balls in place after each exercise.

Circuit Training Exercises General

The exercise reference guide shows examples of basic exercises which can be used to construct a circuit training session. It is important to follow a 'Whole Body Approach' and to vary the body area exercised.

Use an acronym to select your exercises i.e.
B.A.L.S. = Back - Arms - Legs - Stomach

Back - Back Extensions
Arms and shoulders - Triceps Dips, Press Ups
Legs - Squats
Stomach - Half Sit ups.

These are variations of exercises to ensure that players gain maximum benefits and do not become bored with the session. You should visit classes and observe other fitness professionals to increase your exercise vocabulary

Press Ups - Improves Upper Body Strength

Full Press Up
Body position:
Palms of the hands and the toes should touch the ground with the hands shoulder width apart.
Body should be straight with the head in line with the body.
Do not lock out the elbows.

Exercise movement:
First movement - bend the arms and lower the chest to the ground while keeping the body straight
Second movement - straighten the arms and lift the body without locking out at the elbows while keeping the body straight.

Three Quarter Press Up
Body position:
Hands shoulder width apart.
Body straight with head in line with the body
Do not lock out the elbows.
The palms of the hands, the knees and the toes should touch the ground.

Exercise movement:
First movement - bend the arms and lower the chest to the ground while keeping the body straight
Second movement - straighten the arms and lift the body without locking out at the elbow while keeping the body straight.

Box Press Up
Body position:
Hands shoulder width apart.
Body straight with head in line with the body and do not lock out the elbows.
The palms of the hands, the knees (which should be bent to 90 degrees) and the toes, should all be touching the ground.

Exercise movement:
First movement - bend the arms and lower the chest to the ground while keeping the body straight
Second movement - straighten the arms, lift the body without locking out the elbows while keeping the body straight.

Press Up Against a Wall or Incline
Body position:
Hands shoulder width apart.
Body straight with head in line with the body
Do not lock out the elbows.
The palms of the hands should touch the wall or incline; the legs are straight with the feet on the ground.

Exercise movement:
First movement - bend the arms until the chest touches the wall or incline while keeping the body straight
Second movement - straighten the arms, lift the body without locking out at the elbows while keeping the body straight.

Sit Ups - Improves Abdominal Strength

Normal Half Sit Up
Body position:
Lie on the ground facing up.
Knees bent.
Feet flat on the ground
Head in line with the body on the ground.
Hands on the thighs.

Exercise movement:
First movement - Raise the head and shoulders off the ground, sliding the hands until they touch the knees
Second movement - Lower the head and shoulders back to the ground under control.

Half Sit Up with Hands Across the Chest
Body position:
Lie on the ground facing up.
Knees bent.
Feet flat on the ground
Head in line with the body on the ground.
Hands on the chest.

Exercise movement:
First movement - Raise the head and shoulders off the ground, keeping the hands across the chest until they touch the knees.
Second movement - Lower the head and shoulders back to the ground under control.

Half Sit Up with Hands on the Temple
Body position:
Lie on the ground facing up.
Knees bent.
Feet flat on the ground
Head in line with the body on the ground.
Hands on the temple.

Exercise movement:
First movement - Raise the head and shoulders off the ground, keeping the hands touching the temple to a sitting up position.
Second movement - Lower the head and shoulders back to the ground under control.

Half Sit Up Holding a Ball to the Chest
Body position:
Lie on the ground facing up.
Knees bent.
Feet flat on the ground.
Head in line with the body on the ground.
Hands holding the ball to the chest.

Exercise movement:
First movement - Raise the head and shoulders off the ground to a sitting up position.
Second movement - Lower the head and shoulders back to the ground under control.

Crunches - Improves Abdominal Strength

Crunches
Body position:
Lie on the ground facing up with legs bent and feet off the ground.
Hands either on the thighs, chest or resting on the temples.

Exercise movement:
First movement - Raise the head and shoulders and knees at the same time bringing them together.

Crunches with a Twist
Body position:
Lie on the ground facing up with legs bent and feet off the ground.
Hands touching the temples with elbows facing forward.

Exercise movement:
First movement - Raise the head and shoulders and knees at the same time bringing them together, alternately taking the elbow to the opposite knee.

Side Bends - Improves upper body strength

Side Bends Basic
Body position:
Stand with legs hip width apart and knees slightly bent. Hands by the side. Keep the body upright as though fixed between two boards.

Exercise movement:
First movement - Lower the body and take the right hand to the right knee and then revert to an upright position.

Second movement - Lower the body and take the left hand to left knee and then revert to the upright position.

Side Bends Standing Advanced

Body position:
Stand up with the feet positioned hip width apart with the knees slightly bent. Hand on shoulders or above the head. Body upright as though fixed between two boards.

Exercise movement:
First movement - Lower the body to the right side keeping hands in position and then revert to the standing position.
Second movement - Lower the body to the left side keeping hands in position and then revert to the standing position.

Back Extensions - Improves Strength in the Lumbar Area

Back Extensions with Elbows on the Ground

Body position:
Lie face down on the ground with legs straight and on the ground.
Elbows should be bent with the forearms on the ground keeping the head straight.

Exercise movement:
First movement - Raise the chest off the ground ensuring that the forearms stay in contact with the ground.
Second movement - lower the body to the ground in a controlled movement.

Back Extensions with Hands on the Lower Back

Body position:
Lie face down on the ground with legs straight and on the ground.
The arms should be behind the back with hands on the lower back keeping the head straight.

Exercise movement:
First movement - Raise the chest off the ground.
Second movement - lower the body to the ground in a controlled movement.

Back Extensions with Arms Out to the Side
Body position:
Lie face down on the ground with legs straight and on the ground.
The arms should be placed out to the side with elbows bent to 90 degrees flat on the ground keeping the head straight.

Exercise movement:
First movement - Raise the chest and arms off the ground.
Second movement - lower the body to the ground in a controlled movement.

Back Extensions with Hands on the Head
Body position:
Lie face down on the ground with legs straight and on the ground.
The hands should be placed on the temples keeping the head straight.

Exercise movement:
First movement - Raise the chest off the ground. Keep elbows back.
Second movement - lower the body to the ground in a controlled movement.

Back Extensions with Hands Above the Head
Body position:
Lie face down on the ground with legs straight and on the ground.
The hands and arms should be above the head keeping the head straight.

Exercise movement:
First movement - Raise the chest off the ground.
Second movement - lower the body to the ground in a controlled movement.

Squat Thrust - General All Round Strength

Squat Thrust
Body position:
Palms of the hands and the toes should touch the ground with the hands shoulder width apart.
Body should be straight with the head in line with the body.

Exercise movement:
First movement - Jump both feet forward so that the knees are in line with the elbows.
Second movement - Jump both feet back and ensure that the legs are straight.

Squat Thrust using Alternate Legs
Body position:
Palms of the hands and the toes should touch the ground with the hands shoulder width apart.
Body should be straight with the head in line with the body.

Exercise movement:
First movement - Jump one foot forward so that the knee is in line with the elbow.
Second movement - Jump the forward leg back ensuring that the leg is straight while the other leg jumps forward so that the knee is in line with the elbow.

Standing Squat Thrust (Burpee)
Body position:
Start in standing position then go down to the ground with the palms of the hands and the toes touching the ground with the hands shoulder width apart.
Body should be straight with the head in line with the body.

Exercise movement:
First movement - From the standing position go to the squat.
Second movement - Jump both feet back and ensure that the legs are straight.
Third movement - Jump both feet forward so that the knees are in line with the elbows.
Fourth movement - Return to a standing position.

Triceps Dips - Improves strength in the arms and shoulders

Triceps Dips on the ground
Body position:
Sit down with hands and arms behind the body with the hands on the ground, keeping the body straight with the knees bent.

Exercise movement:
First movement - Bend arms and lower the body to the ground.
Second movement - straighten the arms.

Triceps Dips with Hands on a Box: Basic
Body position:
Sit down in front of the box with hands and arms behind the body and the hands on the box with arms bent.
Keep the body straight with the knees bent.

This method allows aid from the legs to perform the movement

Exercise movement:
First movement - Bend arms and lower the body, staying close to the box.
Second movement - Straighten the arms.

Triceps Dips Hands on a Box: Advanced
Body position:
Sit down in front of the box with hands and arms behind the body and the hands on the box with arms bent.
Keep the body and legs straight.

Exercise movement:
First movement - Bend arms and lower the body to the box.
Second movement - straighten the arms.

This method removes the aid from the legs and concentrates exercise on the arms.

Half Squats - Improves Leg Strength

Half Squat with Arms by the Side
Body position:
Stand with the knees slightly bent and feet hip width apart.
Keep the head up and the arms by the side.

Exercise movement:
First movement - Push the body weight through the heels and
the rear of the body away while lowering the body, making sure
the heels do not leave the ground.
Second movement - Straighten the body to an upright position.

Half Squat with Arms on the Chest
Body position:
Stand with the knees slightly bent and feet hip width apart.
Keep the head up and the arms folded across the chest.

Exercise movement:
First movement - Push the body weight through the heels and
the rear of the body away while lowering the body, making sure
the heels do not leave the ground.
Second movement - Straighten the body to an upright position.

Half Squat with Arms in Front
Body position:
Stand with the knees slightly bent and feet hip width apart.
Keep the head up and the arms straight out in front.

Exercise movement:
First movement - Push the body weight through the heels and
the rear of the body away while lowering the body, making sure
the heels do not leave the ground.
Second movement - Straighten the body to an upright position.

Half Squat with Arms in Front While Holding a Ball
Body position:
Stand with the knees slightly bent and feet hip width apart.
Keep the head up and the arms straight out in front with hands
holding a ball.

Exercise movement:
First movement - Push the body weight through the heels and
the rear of the body away while lowering the body, making sure
the heels do not leave the ground.
Second movement - Straighten the body to an upright position.

One Legged Half Squat
Body position:
Stand on one leg with the knee slightly bent and the other leg
stretched out in front.
Keep the head up and the arms by the side.

Exercise movement:
First movement - Push the body weight through the heels of
one leg and the rear of the body away while lowering the body
making sure the heel of that leg does not leave the ground.
Second movement - Straighten the body to an up right position.

Tuck Jump
Body position:
Adopt a standing position with feet hip width apart and arms
slightly bent and over the head.

Exercise movement:
Jump up and bring both knees to the chest and push down with
the arms. Land on both feet at the same time with the knees
bent.

Arm Punching

Body position:

Stand with the knees slightly bent and feet hip width apart.
Keep the head up and the arms straight out in front.

Exercise movement:

Push the arms alternately out straight in front. The movement
should be fast and strong, switch one arm going out as the
other comes back.

Bench Jump

Body position:

Stand with the knees slightly bent and feet hip width apart on
either side of the bench.
Keep the head up and the arms down by the side.

Exercise movement:

Jump with both feet onto the bench at the same time and return
with both feet to the side of the bench. The movement should
fast and strong.

Step Ups

Body position:

Stand with the feet hip width apart in front of the bench.
Keep the head up and the arms down by the side.

Exercise movement:

Step up onto the bench with one leg and straighten the leg,
bringing the other leg on to the bench. Step down leading with
same leg as in the step up, returning to the starting position.
The movement should be strong and the body should be
straightened out when both feet are on the bench.

Trunk Twist
Body position:
Adopt a sitting position with legs astride and have a ball placed between the legs. Hold the ball with both hands.

Exercise movement:
While holding the ball in the hands touch the ball on the ground first outside of the right leg then between the legs and then outside the left leg back to the center. Only twist from the trunk.

Star Jump
Body position:
Stand with the knees slightly bent and feet together.
Keep the head up and the arms down by the side.

Exercise movement:
Jump in the air stretching both arms and legs out to the side creating a star with the body The movement should be fast and strong with both the arms and the legs moving at the same time.

Press Ups
Body position:
The body should be face down with the hands on the ground and the arms fully stretched.
The body should be kept straight at all times with only the toes and the hands touching the ground.

Exercise movement:
The arms should bend so that the face comes close to the ground or an object such as a ball. The arms should then be straightened out until the arms are perfectly straight. The movement should be strong with both the arms moving at the same time.

Soccer Conditioning Games General

Pure fitness training, although very essential, can be and often is boring. Most soccer players would prefer just to play a soccer game, and naturally playing a soccer game will bring a certain amount of fitness. But when players become tired they will just stop and walk.

Introducing a soccer game with a set fitness aim will achieve a higher fitness level. The conditioning game can be made competitive, therefore players will tend to work harder. If your players do not want to win, then you have a problem.

Use the conditioning games not only in preseason fitness but also throughout your season training.

Keep each game to an allocated time of 15 to 20 minutes, depending on the age and fitness of the players.

The aim of the conditioning games is the progressive development of cardiovascular fitness and the muscular system to achieve all-round fitness.

Conditioning games should be fun and enjoyable and should always be performed in teams of different numbers of players.

Conditioning Games

		Equipment needed and the layout of the Training Sessions:
1.	Two vs two in the penalty area	
2.	Three vs three and three Off	
3.	Clear the field	- Use where possible the standard soccer field
4.	Three vs three vs three	
5.	Out gunned	- A stop watch when a specific time for the game is allocated.
6.	End zone	
7.	All change	
8.	Quick fire	- At least one ball between two players.
9.	Triangles	- First aid bag in case of injuries.
10.	Shooting gallery	

Two vs two in the penalty area

Game Objectives:

Two teams of 2 players play against each within the penalty area, with the aim of scoring into the same goal. The team that has ball possession can score while the team without possession must defend.

Layout Description:

Use a goal and penalty area with cones placed around the edge of the penalty area.

Place 2 cones on the intersection of the D with the penalty area.

In the D collect 5 balls before each sequence.

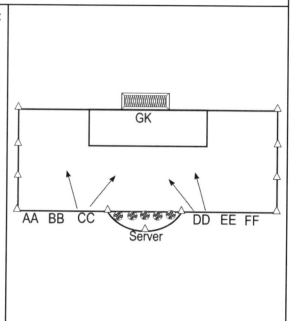

Game Sequence:

The server selects 2 teams by number and plays the ball anywhere into the penalty area. The 2 teams play to obtain possession of the ball and try to score a goal. When a goal is scored or the ball goes out of the penalty area another ball is played in by the server. When all 5 balls have been played the server collects the balls together and selects another 2 teams.

Fitness Record	
Date :	
Players Team AA	Goals Scored
Players Team BB	Goals Scored
Players Team CC	Goals Scored
Players Team DD	Goals Scored
Players Team EE	Goals Scored
Players Team FF	Goals Scored

Comments and Variations:

The players not involved in the game should collect the balls when they go out of play.
Set a maximum time limit for each sequence and rotate the teams so that each team plays against each other.

Three vs three and three off

Game Objectives:

Each team has three attempts to score a goal without goal-keepers. The teams must stay inside their half of the field and are only allowed up to three touches on the ball before shooting. The opposing team should prevent the other team from shooting by using good defensive positioning.

Layout Description:

Create a small-sided field of 40 X 40 yards with a goal at each end.

Create a center line using cones, when possible of another color to that which is used to mark the field.

Use the whole team divided into groups of three players.

If there is an odd number of players rotate the player.

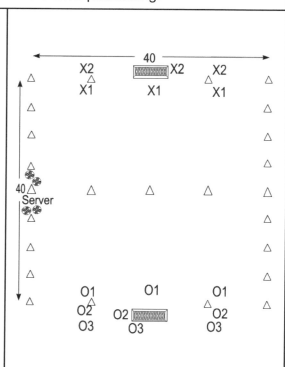

Game Sequence:

The server plays the ball alternately to the X teams or O teams. Each team has three attempts to score a goal, then the next team of 3 players comes on. If the ball crosses the halfway line the opposing team has the ball. If the ball goes out of the playing area then the server plays another ball to the opposite team that caused the ball to go out of the playing area.

Fitness Record	
Date:	Time Allocation:
Team X1 Players	No. of goals
Team X2 Players	No. of goals
Team O1 Players	No. of goals
Team O2 Players	No. of goals
Team O3 Players	No. of goals

Comments and Variations:

Keep the ball in play where possible.
Try where possible to create an odd number of teams so that there is a rotation of teams playing each other.

A time limit can be set for each team to score as many goals as possible before the team is changed out.

The teams should run to the opposite end when they are finished, ready to play from that end.

Clear the field

Game Objectives:

Pass the ball into space in the opposing half of the field. The teams must prevent a ball from going dead or stopping in their half. If one of the balls goes dead i.e. stops moving or goes outside of the playing area, the opposing team gains a point.

Layout Description:

Set out a grid 20 X 20 yards with cones and a center line to divide the field.

If possible use another colored cone for the center line to that which is used to mark the grid.

Use a maximum of four players for each team and two teams to each grid.

Start with 2 balls to a grid, 1 in either half.

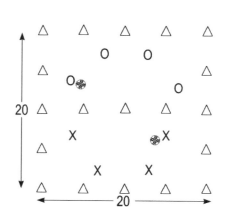

Game Sequence:

The players only have a maximum of two touches, 'one to control and one to pass' the ball. The players may not cross the half way line. Start with two balls and add more balls as required to increase intensity. On the command 'GO' the balls should be passed into an area unoccupied by the opposing team players in the opposite half of the playing area.

Fitness Record	
Date: Time allocation:	
X Team Players	Number of Points
O Team Players	Number of Points
X Team Players	Number of Points
O Team Players	Number of Points

Comments and Variations:

Start with a maximum of five minutes with a break of two minutes and then a further five minutes of play.
Increase the playing time as players get fitter, but the winning
points should not increase significantly as both teams should
not allow the ball to go dead.

Using more than 2 balls requires more concentration and may
become confusing at first, but try to introduce up to 4 balls at
one time.

Three vs three vs three

Game Objectives:

The team without possession must regain ball possession. Create three teams one being a 'rogue team' who always plays with the team which has possession of the ball.

Layout Description:

Set out a grid 30 X 30 yards with cones.

Set out enough grids to accommodate the whole team.

Use a maximum of nine players to a grid.

The size of the area depends on the fitness of the players. A large area creates more space and makes possession of the ball more difficult to regain.

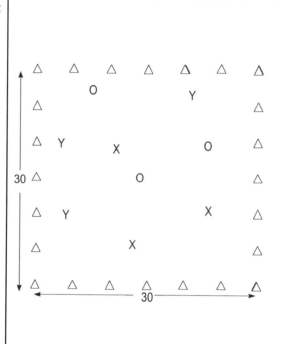

Game Sequence:

The X and O players play against each other to obtain possession of the ball. When the X players have possession of the ball the Y 'rogue team' plays with the X players. As soon as the O players regain possession the Y 'rogue team' switches sides to play with the O players. Rotate the rogue team every two minutes. If the ball is kicked out of the playing area then the opposing team kicks the ball back into play.

Fitness Record

Date: Time Allocation:

Team O Players

Team X Players

Team Y Players

Team O Players

Team X Players

Team Y Players

Comments and Variations:

If not enough players are available then reduce the number of players in the 'rogue team'. This is very intensive practice so work with a small time allocation e.g. two to three minutes, but make sure that the players are working hard. As players get fitter the time can be increased, but the intensity and concentration must not decrease.

Out gunned

Game Objectives:

The object of the game is to have all 5 players of one team in the opposing half of the field. Players must pass the ball into the other half and have it returned by a team player. If the forward and return pass are successful then one player can move into the opposing half.

Layout Description:

Set out a grid 40 X 20 yards with cones and lay out a center line at 20 yards to divide the field.

Where possible, use a different colored cone for the center line to that which is used to mark the grid.

Use up to a maximum of five players for each team and a maximum of ten players to one grid.

Set up each team to start with four players in one half and one in the opposing half.

Game Sequence:
Start with the ball in one half of the field and have the team play the ball between them, three times before the ball can be passed to the forward player. The forward player creates space to receive the ball and passes it back to create the forward and pass back situation. A player may then run into the opposing half to establish two players in the opposing half. The opposing team must prevent the pass and set up their own passing opportunity.

Fitness Record
Date: Time Allocation:
Team O: Number of times Out Gunned:
Team X: Number of times Out Gunned:
Team O: Number of times Out Gunned:
Team X: Number of times Out Gunned:

Comments and Variations:

The forward player or players must create space to receive a pass while the back players must create passing angles and options.
Set a time limit for the game but if one team is too strong change some of the players around.

End zones

Game Objectives:

The object is to score points in one of the 'End Zones'. To score a player must enter an 'End Zone' with the ball. Each 'End Zone' has a different point value e.g. 1, 2 or 3 with 3 being the goal area.

Layout Description:

Use the whole soccer field divided into 3 zones.

Set out the two end zone areas using cones across the field in line with the top of the goal area. Set out 5 sub-zones with sub-zone 1 from the side-line to the penalty area line and sub-zone 2 being the penalty area line to the goal area line. Sub-zone 3 is the goal area.

Create a center zone with cones of 10 yards either side of the center line.

Use maximum of 16 players, eight to a team.

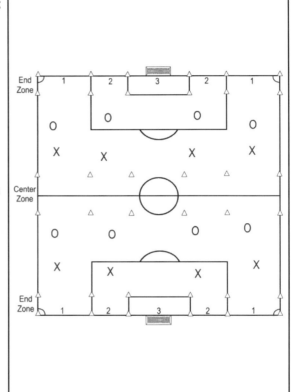

Game Sequence:

The starting team must start with a minimum of three passes before passing over the center zone to an attacking player. The receiving attacking player must pass the ball back into the center zone for a defender to collect and join the attacking players to score points in the end zone. The play remains live until the ball goes out of play or is dead through scoring points in the end zone. Restart with the opposing team passing at least three passes in the defending area.

Fitness Record
Date: Time Allocation:
Team O players   Points
Team X Players   Points

Comments and Variations:

If the team with possession loses the ball while in attack and they have an additional player in the attacking half, then this player must return to the defensive half. Only 1 extra player is allowed in the attacking half while that team has possession at any one time.

All change

Game Objectives:

The attacking team must keep possession of the ball until all members of their team except 1 player are in the attacking half of the field. The aim is to score as many consecutive attacks as possible, gaining a point for each attack.

Layout Description:

Use the whole field without any cones.

Practice with a maximum of 16 players at one time.

One player from each team must stay in the defending half when the rest of the team has moved to the attacking half.

Game Sequence:
Both teams except one player from each team start in one half of the field. Start with an X team player passing the ball into the attacking half. The attacking team must keep possession of the ball until all attacking team players except one are in the attacking half, which will score a point. Players are only allowed up to two touches of the ball before passing. If possession is lost then the opponents become the attacking team and they attack in the same direction. The play remains live until the ball goes out of play. Restart with a short pass from the team that did not put the ball out of play.

Fitness Record

Date: Time Allocation:

Team O Players: Points:

Team X Players   Points:

Comments and Variations:

Set a time limit for the game but if one team is too strong change some of the players around to make it more even.

When a team has all players except 1 in the attacking half they turn around and attack in the opposite direction. This will make a mismatch of players and can become confusing.

Quick fire

Game Objectives:

The first player to the ball becomes the attacker. The attacking player must try to score while the defender must win back possession of the ball without fouling the attacker.

Layout Description:

Use half of the field and the goal and penalty area with cones placed around the half field.

Place two cones in line with the penalty area 10 yards and 20 yards from the top of the penalty area.

This will mark where the players start and where the server kicks the ball into play.

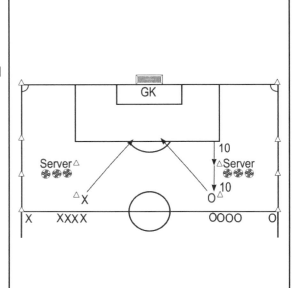

Game Sequence:

Use two players at one time starting facing away from the goal. On the command 'GO' both players turn and sprint to collect the ball from the server and the one who receives the ball first becomes the attacker and attempts to shoot to score a goal. Both players should make a recovery run around the outside of cones and collect the ball, while the next two players proceed with the practice. Use different ball deliveries: high balls, bouncing balls, low balls, short passes, long passes and throws. For variations of play, use two vs two or two vs one. Introduce a passive defender in the penalty area whom the attacking player must shoot around.

Fitness Record

Date:

Player Name   Goals

Comments and Variations:

If the ball goes out of the playing area the sequence is finished and the next two players start.

Try to pair players of similar ability.

Triangles

Game Objectives:

This is Interval training to simulate closing down an opposing player and recovery with the ball. The players must pass the ball and sprint for 10 yards, sprint to close down an opponent and dribble the ball back to the start.

Layout Description:	
Set out triangle grids 10 X 10 X 10 yards using cones. Set out enough grids to accommodate the whole team. Use only three players for each grid. Place a ball on cone A of each grid.	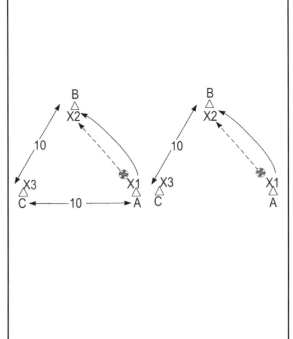

Game Sequence:

On the command 'GO' X1 passes the ball to X2 and then sprints to cone B. X2 plays the ball to X3 and X1 then sprints to cone C and takes the ball from X3 and recovers dribbling the ball to the start cone A. X1 finishes by passing the ball to X2 and X2 becomes the start player and repeats the same sequence. Repeat five to ten times = 1500-3000 yards, depending on the fitness of the players

Fitness Record	
Date:	Allocated group time
Grid players:	Team Grid Laps
Grid players:	Team Grid Laps
Grid players:	Team Grid Laps
Grid players:	Team Grid Laps
Grid players:	Team Grid Laps

Comments and Variations:

Increase the number of sequences as the players become fitter. The players should run on the outside of the cones.

On the second leg, instead of the X2 player passing to X3, the X1 player takes the ball from X2 and either juggles or runs backward with the ball to X3. The third leg stays the same as before.

Shooting gallery

Game Objectives:

The aim is to score a goal with a snap shot or improvise. The servers must ensure that a ball is always in the playing area at all times.

Layout Description:

Create a small-sided field of 40 X 40 yards with a goal at each end.

Place a ball at each corner with a server to play the ball when requested.

Use a maximum of eight players plus two goalkeepers and up to four servers or a third team for rotation.

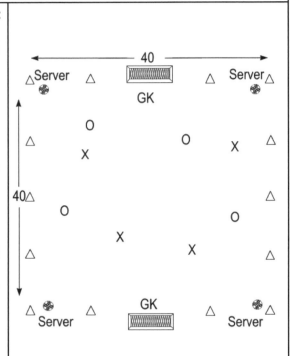

Game Sequence:

The servers take turns playing a ball into space, varying the types of delivery. The players must sprint to the ball and shoot or improvise. The ball stays live until a goal is scored or the ball is out of play. When the ball is out of play a server introduces a new ball quickly. Make a time allocation for switching around the teams. If the goalkeeper saves a shot he throws the ball to one of his players.

Fitness Record		
Date:	Time Allocation:	
Team players / Goals:		
O	X	S
O	X	S
O	X	S
O	X	S
O	X	S
Team players / Goals:		
O	X	S
O	X	S
O	X	S
O	X	S
O	X	S
Team players / Goals:		
O	X	S
O	X	S
O	X	S
O	X	S
O	X	S
Team players / Goals:		
O	X	S
O	X	S
O	X	S
O	X	S
O	X	S

Comments and Variations:

The players can be limited to a number of touches but do not allow more than three touches before the ball is passed or shot. Use a different colored shirt for each team, including the server team

Goalkeeping Fitness Training General

Functional Attributes:

Agility	Fast directional changes	Speed over short distances
Timing	Balance	Jumping static leg power
Landing	coordination	Reaction, fast foot-work.

Rapid acceleration and deceleration

The Goalkeepers Role:

The Goalkeeper has an excellent view of the playing field and is therefore able to read the game and direct players accordingly to adapt to the different situations developing in front of him. Therefore, good communication skills are essential.

The Goalkeeper is also the originator of fast attacking play through good distribution of the ball into wide areas.
The Goalkeeper is often an extrovert type not afraid to order the players in front when they are not performing correctly, ensuring that the defensive unit works in harmony.

The Goalkeeper must be able to make fast, directional changes in order to react to the movement of the ball across the goal and be able to dive to make a save.
Preventing and stopping shots requires great agility and strength and the Goalkeeper requires good static leg power to be able to project himself across the goal to make a crucial save.
Since the introduction of the back pass rule the Goalkeeper must now be able to accelerate out to the edge of the goal area, to either clear a back pass or deal with a direct threat from a through ball or a one on one situation.

Goalkeeper Training Sessions:

These training sessions are designed specifically to be used for Goalkeepers and each exercise can be used as a test to evaluate the fitness progress of goalkeepers by timing and recording a specific movement.

The exercises can also be used to train goalkeepers by using several different sessions with different repetitions in a circuit.

1.	Dealing with the chip shot
2.	Dealing with a low shot
3.	Dealing with the back-pass
4.	Movement across the goalmouth
5.	Pick up and throw
6.	Speed off the goal line
7.	Dealing with rebounds
8.	Static jumping
9.	Static diving
10.	Jumping to punch the ball

Equipment needed and the layout of the Training Sessions:

- A set of cones for marking the training area.

- A long tape measure for setting the distances for the training layout.

- A stop watch for evaluating the fitness of the players.

- At least one ball between two players.

- First aid bag in case of injuries.

All sessions are laid out in and around the penalty area to keep the perspective on the goal wherever possible.

Dealing with the chip shot

Fitness Aims:

To develop the ability of goalkeepers to deal with chip shots. This session should improve the speed of backward movement and the agility to prevent a goal and deal with the ball.

Layout Description:

Set up Gate (A) and (B) on the penalty area line either side of the D as the starting positions.

Set up Gate (C) as a box (2 X 2 yards) centrally on the goal line as the finishing position.

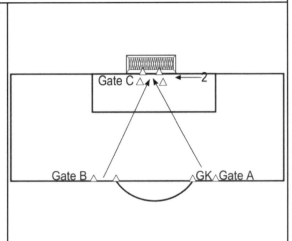

Organization:

The goalkeeper starts with his back to the goal and both feet on the edge of the penalty area. On the command 'GO' the goalkeeper runs backwards from gate (A) to gate (C). Once inside gate (C) the goalkeeper should jump to touch the crossbar with either hand, simulating a save by tipping over the bar. Alternate the start position between Gate (A and B).

System of measurement:

Time the movement from gate (A) 'GO' to the hand contact with the crossbar

Fitness Record

Date: Goalkeeper Name:
Time from cone (A) to touching the crossbar:

Date: Goalkeeper Name:
Time from cone (B) to touching the crossbar:

Date: Goalkeeper Name:
Time from cone (A) to touching the crossbar:

Date: Goalkeeper Name:
Time from cone (B) to touching the crossbar:

Date: Goalkeeper Name:
Time from cone (A) to touching the crossbar:

Date: Goalkeeper Name:
Time from cone (B) to touching the crossbar:

Training Variations:

Starting positions can be adjusted to suit the needs of the session and the ability of the players. The gates can be moved to the corners of the penalty area to create a longer run.

This could also be used as a repetition session where the goalkeeper runs backwards from Gate (A) to Gate (C) to touch the crossbar and then runs on to Gate (B) to repeat the action. Measure the number of times the goalkeeper touches the crossbar per minute.

Dealing with a low shot

Fitness Aims:

To develop the goalkeeper's ability to deal with low shots.
This session should improve the speed and agility to prevent a
goal or recover.

Layout Description: Use the goal and goal area box to set up this session. Place cones (A and B) on the corners of the goal area. This is the start posi- tion. Place a ball at the foot of each goal post for the end position.	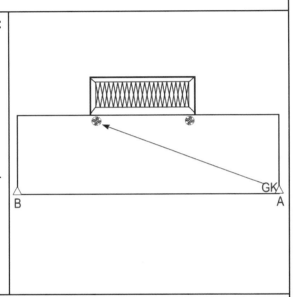

Organization:

The goalkeeper starts with both feet on the lines marking the
corner of the goal area at cone (A). On the command 'GO' the
goalkeeper runs diagonally across the six-yard box to dive and
place both hands on the stationary ball at the opposite goal
post. While the goalkeeper is running he should keep his eye
on the other corner of the penalty area. Alternate the start position between (A and B).

System of measurement:

Time the movement from the command 'GO' to player having
both hands on the ball.

Fitness Record

Date: Goalkeeper Name:
Time from cone (A) to the ball

Date: Goalkeeper Name:
Time from cone (B) to the ball

Date: Goalkeeper Name:
Time from cone (A) to the ball

Date: Goalkeeper Name:
Time from cone (B) to the ball

Date: Goalkeeper Name:
Time from cone (A) to the ball

Date: Goalkeeper Name:
Time from cone (B) to the ball

Training Variations:

This could also be used as a repetition session where the goalkeeper starts at cone (A) and runs diagonally across the six-yard box to dive and place both hands on the stationary ball at the opposite goal post. The goalkeeper then runs to cone (B) to repeat the action in the opposite direction.

Count the number of times the goalkeeper makes the diagonal run across the six-yard box to dive and place both hands on the stationary ball at the opposite goal post in 1 minute.

Dealing with the back-pass

Fitness Aims:

To train the goalkeeper to deal with a back pass.
This session should develop acceleration and speed of movement and how to move quickly and deal with the ball from a back pass.

Layout Description:

Set out a cone on the middle of the edge of the goal area (A).
This is the start position.

Set out a series of cones on the penalty area. Set 1 cone at each corner of the penalty area and 1 in the middle.
Set 2 further cones each 5 yards outside the intersection of the D area.

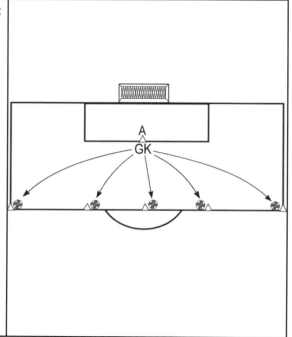

Organization:

The goalkeeper starts with both feet on the edge of the goal area with 1 foot touching cone (A). On the command 'GO' the goalkeeper runs forward from cone (A) and strikes 1 of the balls and kicks it up the field. The goalkeeper should then run backwards keeping an eye on where the ball has gone until he reaches the cone (A) touching it with 1 foot.

System of measurement:

Time the movement from cone (A) 'GO' to striking the ball and returning to cone (A).

Fitness Record

Date: Goalkeeper Name:
Time from cone (A) to kicking the ball
a.   at the corner of the penalty area:
b.   at 5 yards from the intersection of the D:
c.   in the middle of the penalty area:

Date: Goalkeeper Name:
Time from cone (A) to kicking the ball
a.   at the corner of the penalty area:
b.   at 5 yards from the intersection of the D:
c.   in the middle of the penalty area:

Date: Goalkeeper Name:
Time from cone (A) to kicking the ball
a.   at the corner of the penalty area:
b.   at 5 yards from the intersection of the D:
c.   in the middle of the penalty area:

Training Variations:

This can be a timed test of the movement between cone (A) and kicking one ball, or used as a fitness drill which is timed with the goalkeeper moving between cone (A) and kicking all balls or as many balls as possible in a given time.

Movement across the goalmouth

Fitness Aims:

To train the goalkeeper to move across the goalmouth at speed. The session should develop agile feet for speed of sideways movement across the goal and collect the ball.

Layout Description:	
Set up cones on the edge of the goal area opposite each goal post for 2 servers. Place a ball at each server position. The goalkeeper must start centrally 1 yard in front of the goal line.	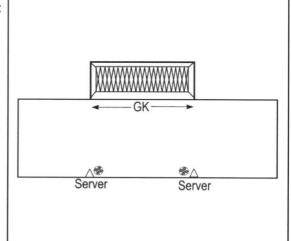

Organization:

The goalkeeper starts centrally with both feet in front of the goal line. On the command 'GO' the player moves laterally across the goalmouth. When the goalkeeper reaches the post the server delivers the ball, which should be caught and returned to the server before moving to the opposite post where the action is repeated.

System of measurement:

Count how many catches the player makes in 1 minute from the command 'GO'

Fitness Record

Date: Goalkeeper Name:
Number of catches in 1 minute:

Date: Goalkeeper Name:
Number of catches in 1 minute:

Date: Goalkeeper Name:
Number of catches in 1 minute:

Date: Goalkeeper Name:
Number of catches in 1 minute:

Date: Goalkeeper Name:
Number of catches in 1 minute:

Date: Goalkeeper Name:
Number of catches in 1 minute:

Date: Goalkeeper Name:
Number of catches in 1 minute:

Training Variations:

A second variation is to use 1 server but with enough balls to keep the session going.

The ball deliveries can be varied to suit the needs of the session. These deliveries can be high into the corner or low on the ground.

Pick up and throw

Fitness Aims:

To train the goalkeeper to receive and distribute the ball by throwing to a wide position. The session should develop reactions and coordination to set up attacking play.

Layout Description:

Use the goal and penalty areas. Tthe goalkeeper start position is in the center on the goal line cone (A).

Set up 4 cones on the edge of the goal area, 1 on each corner and 1 each inline with the goal posts. Place a ball on each cone.

Place cones in well spaced out positions for players to receive the ball.

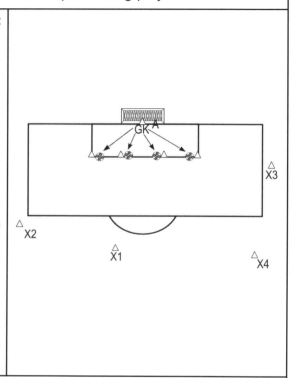

Organization:

The goalkeeper starts with both feet on the goal line at cone (A). On the command 'GO' the goalkeeper runs from cone (A) to the edge of the goal area where he should pick up 1 of the balls and execute an over-arm throw to a wide positioned player on the field.

System of measurement:

Time the movement from the goal line, on the command 'GO', to the release of the ball.

Fitness Record

Date: Goalkeeper Name:
Time from cone (A) to throwing the ball
a. at the corner of the goal area:
b. in line with the goal post:

Date: Goalkeeper Name:
Time from cone (A) to throwing the ball
a. at the corner of the goal area:
b. in line with the goal post:

Date: Goalkeeper Name:
Time from cone (A) to throwing the ball
a. at the corner of the goal area:
b. in line with the goal post:

Date: Goalkeeper Name:
Time from cone (A) to throwing the ball
a. at the corner of the goal area:
b. in line with the goal post:

Training Variations:

A second variation is where the goalkeeper throws the first ball and kicks the second ball, but measure the time from `GO` until the second ball is kicked.

This could also be used as a repetition session where the goalkeeper runs to each cone, picks up 1 of the balls and executes an over-arm throw to a wide positioned player.
Each time the goalkeeper must return to cone (A) before going to the next ball.
Measure the time taken from the command `GO` to throwing the last ball.

Speed off the goal line

Fitness Aims:

Develop the speed of the goalkeeper in order to deal with a one on one attacking player. This session should develop agility and speed in both forward and diagonal movement.

Layout Description:

The goalkeeper's start position is in the middle of the goal on the goal line cone (A).

Set up 1 cone on each corner of the goal area and 1 on the penalty spot.

Place 2 more cones in line with the goal area and 2 yards inside the penalty area.
Place a ball at each cone.

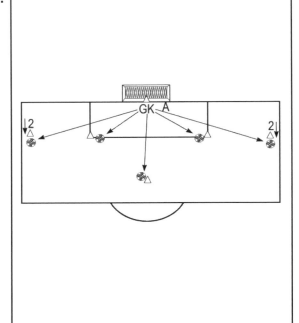

Organization:

The goalkeeper starts with both feet on the goal line at cone (A). On the command 'GO' the player runs from the goal line to place both hands on and behind the ball in a side lying position. The cones can be adjusted to suit the requirements of the session and the ability of the goalkeeper.

System of measurement:

Time the movement from leaving the goal line, on the command 'GO', to the goalkeeper lying on the side with both hands stationary on the ball.

Fitness Record

Date: Goalkeeper Name:
Time from cone (A) to the ball
a. at the corner of the goal area:
b. on the penalty spot:
c. at the side of the penalty area:

Date: Goalkeeper Name:
Time from cone (A) to the ball
a. at the corner of the goal area:
b. on the penalty spot:
c. at the side of the penalty area:

Date: Goalkeeper Name:
Time from cone (A) to the ball
a. at the corner of the goal area:
b. on the penalty spot:
c. at the side of the penalty area:

Training Variations:

A second variation is when a server rolls a ball from the penalty spot to anywhere in the penalty area for the goalkeeper to block in a side lying position with both hands on and behind ball. This would be difficult to measure.

This could also be used as a repetition session where the goalkeeper runs to each cone, adopting a side lying position with both hands on and behind ball. Each time the goalkeeper must return to cone (A) before going to the next ball.
Measure the time taken from the command `GO` to the goalkeeper lying on the side with both hands stationary on the last ball.

Dealing with rebounds

Fitness Aims:

To train the goalkeeper to deal with rebounds and improve lateral movement along the goal line. The session should develop agility and speed of movement.

Layout Description:	
The goalkeeper's start position is in the middle of the goal and on the goal line. Place a ball at the base of each goal post at 1 yard in from the post. Place a cone in the middle and on the edge of goal area.	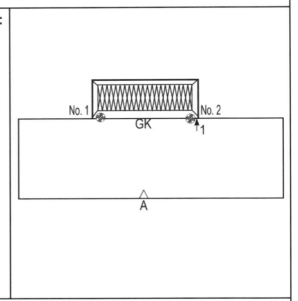

Organization:

The goalkeeper starts with both feet on the goal line in the middle of the goal opposite the marker cone (A). On the command 'GO' the goalkeeper moves laterally and adopts a side lying position with both hands on and behind ball no. 1 and then immediately to adopt the same position with ball no. 2.

System of measurement:

Time the movement from the command 'GO' to the player in a side lying position with both hands on and behind ball no. 2

Fitness Record

Date: Goalkeeper Name:
Time from `GO` to ball No. 1:

Date: Goalkeeper Name:
Time from `GO` to ball No. 2:

Date: Goalkeeper Name:
Time from `GO` to ball No. 1:

Date: Goalkeeper Name:
Time from `GO` to ball No. 2:

Date: Goalkeeper Name:
Time from `GO` to ball No. 1:

Date: Goalkeeper Name:
Time from `GO` to ball No. 2:

Training Variations:

A second variation is when a server rolls a ball to each corner of the goal for the goalkeeper to block in a side lying position with both hands on and behind ball.

This could also be used as a repetition session where the goal-keeper should move side to side, adopting a side lying position with both hands on and behind ball, and count the number of times in 1 minute.

Static jumping

Fitness Aims:

To train the goalkeeper in static jumping and improve take off and landing.
This session will develop leg strength, agility, power, timing and coordination.

Layout Description: This drill requires specialist equipment to measure the goalkeeper's fitness and jumping ability. A wall or marker pole with a scale marked on it is ideal. Alternatively, for a fitness drill, the goalmouth will suffice.	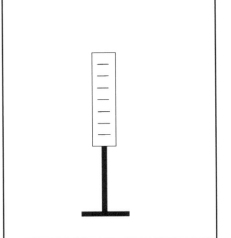

Organization:

Set up a test site using a wall or a vertical marker pole. The player must start parallel to the scale on the wall or marker pole. From a static position the player must jump with one arm extended to touch the highest possible position on the scale. The easiest way to make a mark is for the player to have a piece of chalk in the fingers of the extended hand and to mark the highest point attained.

System of measurement:

Record the height from the floor to the highest point reached by the player.
Record the best of three jumps.

Fitness Record

Date: Goalkeeper Name:
Highest point 1:
Highest point 2:
Highest point 3:

Date: Goalkeeper Name:
Highest point 1:
Highest point 2:
Highest point 3:

Date: Goalkeeper Name:
Highest point 1:
Highest point 2:
Highest point 3:

Date: Goalkeeper Name:
Highest point 1:
Highest point 2:
Highest point 3:

Training Variations:

This test can also be used on other players, not just the goal-keeper.

If only a goal is available then the player should stand next to the goal post and jump as high as possible, using the crossbar as a reference.

As a drill the player should run along the goal line jumping to touch the top of the crossbar 3 to 4 times both forwards and backwards

Static diving

Fitness Aims:

To train the goalkeeper in static diving.
The session should develop power, agility and coordination.

Layout Description:	
Place a ball and a cone in line with the goal post. Set up a series of cones over a meas-ured distance from the ball e.g. one-foot apart, in front of the goal. The first cone should be the dis-tance of the height of the goalkeeper. If the diving surface is too hard a mat should be used.	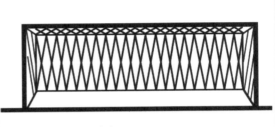 

Organization:

The goalkeeper starts at the nearest cone and performs a dive to place his hands on and behind the ball. The distance of the dive should be increased a foot at a time until the goalkeeper is very close to the maximum distance and then increased in inch-es. The goalkeeper should aim to increase the distance of the dive until he can no longer place both hands on and behind the ball.

System of measurement:

Measure the maximum distance of dive the goalkeeper attains from a static position to place both hands on and behind the ball.

Fitness Record
Date: Goalkeeper Name: Maximum distance:
Date: Goalkeeper Name: Maximum distance:
Date: Goalkeeper Name: Maximum distance:
Date: Goalkeeper Name: Maximum distance:
Date: Goalkeeper Name: Maximum distance:
Date: Goalkeeper Name: Maximum distance:
Date: Goalkeeper Name: Maximum distance:

Training Variations:

This session can be done either standing or crouching for each jump.

When the goalkeeper is at maximum distance with hands on and behind the ball, test the distance where he can still punch the ball out of the goal area.

This is a diving session, so make sure the diving action is correct and the goalkeeper does not get injured.

Jumping To punch the ball

Fitness Aims:

To train the goalkeeper in take off and landing when punching the ball.

The session should develop power, agility, coordination and timing.

Layout Description:

Set up 3 cones on the goal line starting at 2 yards from the goal post and 2 yards apart from each other.

Create jumping obstacles using cones and sticks placed 1 yard in front of each cone with the following heights:
- 1 ½ feet
- 2 feet
- 2 ½ feet.

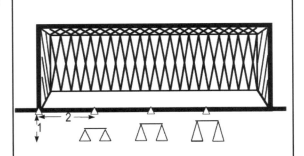

Organization:

The goalkeeper stands next to the cone on the goal line and jumps as far as he can using 1 foot and landing on the other side of the cone obstacle. The goalkeeper should try to obtain the furthest distance for each of the different heights of cone obstacles. The goalkeeper should be encouraged to use an arm action with arms stretched up and out in front at the highest point of the jump.

System of measurement:

Measure the distance from the take off position to the first point of landing for each cone obstacle.

Fitness Record

Date: Goalkeeper Name:
Distance 1:   Distance 2:   Distance 3:

Date: Goalkeeper Name:
Distance 1:   Distance 2:   Distance 3:

Date: Goalkeeper Name:
Distance 1:   Distance 2:   Distance 3:

Date: Goalkeeper Name:
Distance 1:   Distance 2:   Distance 3:

Date: Goalkeeper Name:
Distance 1:   Distance 2:   Distance 3:

Date: Goalkeeper Name:
Distance 1:   Distance 2:   Distance 3:

Date: Goalkeeper Name:
Distance 1:   Distance 2:   Distance 3:

Training Variations:

Use a ball in a net hung from a stick where possible, even if another player holds it. This will make the practice more realistic as the goalkeeper should try to punch the ball.

Utilizing all 3 obstacles the goalkeeper would start jumping over the lowest and ending up finishing at the highest. Between jumping, the goalkeeper should run backwards to the next cone.

Measure the time from the first cone until the last jump.

Defender Fitness Training General

Functional Attributes:

Speed	Timing	Coordination	Agility
Endurance	Strength	Static leg power	

Rapid acceleration and deceleration

The Defender's Role:

The defenders are the last line of players in front of the goal and should through individual play and cohesive unit play offer some protection to the goalkeeper and the goal.

The individual defender must be a good tackler and must have good static leg power to be able to jump and head the ball well.

The defender must have balance and timing to avoid committing infringements in central or near central positions in the defensive third of the playing area.

In addition to balance and timing the defender must have excellent recovery ability combined with speed and acceleration to recover behind the ball if beaten by an opponent.

Wide playing defenders are also required to support attacking play and must have a high level of endurance, to move up to support the play, when their team is in possession of the ball and to recover to a defensive position when possession is lost.

Defender Training Sessions:

These training sessions are designed specifically to be used for defenders and each exercise can be used as a test to evaluate the fitness progress by timing and recording a singular movement.

The exercises can also be used to train defenders by using several different sessions with different reparations in a circuit.

Defender Fitness Training Sessions

1. Recovering and changing direction
2. Recovery when possession is lost
3. Support attack and recovery run
4. Defending at corners and shot blocking
5. Recover and start a new attack
6. Tracking back showing the inside
7. Defending and showing the side line
8. Recovering to execute a tackle
9. Recovery from the ground
10. Diagonal recovery runs

Equipment needed and the layout of the Training Sessions:

⊙ A set of cones for marking the training area.

⊙ A long tape measure for setting the distances for the training layout.

⊙ A stop watch for evaluating the fitness of the players.

⊙ At least one ball between two players.

⊙ First aid bag in case of injuries.

All sessions are laid out in and around the penalty area to keep the perspective on defending the goal wherever possible.

Recovering and changing direction

Fitness Aims:

To train players in defensive movement and changing direction. This session should develop the speed of backward movement and the agility to change direction.

Layout Description:
Use the penalty and goal areas for this session.
Set up 5 cones with Cone (A) level with the corner of penalty area and level with the top edge of the D. Set cone (B) level with penalty spot and level with the corner of the goal area. Cone (C) should be on the edge of D and level with the penalty spot. Set up cones (D and E) the same as (B and A) respectively but on the opposite side.

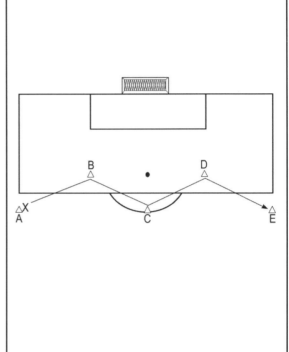

Organization:
The player starts with both feet in contact with cone (A) facing toward the halfway line. On the command 'GO' the player runs between the cones, touching each cone with 1 hand:
Backward from cone (A) to cone (B)
Forward from cone (B) to cone (C)
Backward from cone (C) to cone (D)
Forward from cone (D) to cone (E)

System of measurement:
Time the movement from the command 'GO' to the player touching the last cone (E).

Fitness Record

Date: Player Name:
Time from `GO` to the player touching cone (E):

Date: Player Name:
Time from `GO` to the player touching cone (E):

Date: Player Name:
Time from `GO` to the player touching cone (E):

Date: Player Name:
Time from `GO` to the player touching cone (E):

Date: Player Name:
Time from `GO` to the player touching cone (E):

Date: Player Name:
Time from `GO` to the player touching cone (E):

Date: Player Name:
Time from `GO` to the player touching cone (E):

Date: Player Name:
Time from `GO` to the player touching cone (E):

Training Variations:

This session can be made into a circuit where the players would be timed for an average of 3 runs through the cones

Have all the players run through the cones one after another. Have a player act as the starter and when he drops the hand start the stopwatch, and record each run in a list against the player's name.

Check new results on a regular basis.

Recovery when possession is lost

Fitness Aims:

To train defensive players to recover when possession of the ball is lost to the opposing team.
This session should develop speed, agility and coordination of players.

Layout Description:
Set up three cones in a triangle.

Cone (A) 3 yards in from the sideline and level with the edge of the penalty area.

Cone (B) 3 yards in from the sideline and 20 yards outside of the penalty area in line with cone (A).

Cone (C) 10 yards in from the sideline and equal distance from cones (A and B).

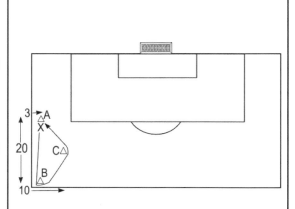

Organization:
The player starts with both feet in contact with cone (A) facing forwards. On the command 'GO' the player runs forward to touch cone (B) with one hand. The player then runs backwards recovering to cone (C) in a defensive stance showing the inside of the field. On reaching cone (C) the player should move in a defensive stance showing outside of the field and recover to cone (A), touching it with a hand.

System of measurement:
Time the movement from the command 'GO' to the player touching cone (A) with one hand.

Fitness Record

Date: Player Name:
Time from `GO` to the player touching cone (A):

Date: Player Name:
Time from `GO` to the player touching cone (A):

Date: Player Name:
Time from `GO` to the player touching cone (A):

Date: Player Name:
Time from `GO` to the player touching cone (A):

Date: Player Name:
Time from `GO` to the player touching cone (A):

Date: Player Name:
Time from `GO` to the player touching cone (A):

Date: Player Name:
Time from `GO` to the player touching cone (A):

Date: Player Name:
Time from `GO` to the player touching cone (A):

Training Variations:

The cones for this session can be set out in longer distances e.g. cone (A) on the end line cone (B) on the half way line with cone (C) placed on the corner of the penalty area.

The session could also be set up to include both options and a player runs through the short layout and then through the long layout.

Support attack and recovery run

Fitness Aims:
To train defensive players to support the attack and to make recovery runs.
This session should develop speed and coordination of defensive players.

Layout Description:
Set up cone (A) 10 yards inside defending half of playing area on the edge of the center circle. This is the start position.

Set up cone (B) on the edge of the penalty area in attacking half of field on the edge of the intersection of the D.

Set up cone (C) at 45-degree angle in line with the penalty area and 15 yards back towards the half way line.

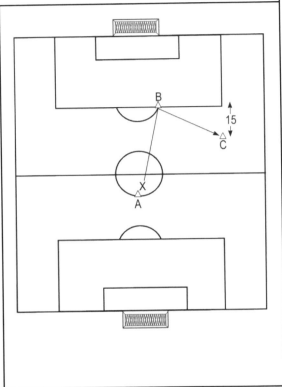

Organization:
The player starts with both feet in contact with cone (A). On the command 'GO' the player runs forward to touch cone (B) with one foot.
The player must then change direction and sprint to cone (C), still keeping an eye on the play. This simulates recovering to challenge the ball delivered to a wide player by the goalkeeper when possession is lost.

System of measurement:
Time the movement from the command 'GO' to the player touching cone (C) with 1 foot.

Fitness Record

Date: Player Name:
Time from `GO` to the player touching cone (C):

Date: Player Name:
Time from `GO` to the player touching cone (C):

Date: Player Name:
Time from `GO` to the player touching cone (C):

Date: Player Name:
Time from `GO` to the player touching cone (C):

Date: Player Name:
Time from `GO` to the player touching cone (C):

Date: Player Name:
Time from `GO` to the player touching cone (C):

Date: Player Name:
Time from `GO` to the player touching cone (C):

Date: Player Name:
Time from `GO` to the player touching cone (C):

Date: Player Name:
Time from `GO` to the player touching cone (C):

Training Variations:

Another cone (D) can be placed on the sideline where the player must run around cone (C) and onto cone (D), simulating a throw from the goalkeeper to the sideline.
Set up the layout on both sides of the field so that players can train both ways.

Defending at corners and shot blocking

Fitness Aims:
To train defensive players to head the ball on corner situations. The player should be able to recover and block shots from the opposing team.
The session should improve the speed, agility and power of the defensive player

Layout Description:
Use the penalty and goal areas for this drill.
The player's start position, cone (A), is on the inside of the near goal post as in defending a corner kick.

Set up cone (B) on corner of the six-yard area.

Position a server on the corner of the penalty area with a ball. This is to deliver a simulated corner kick for player to head away.

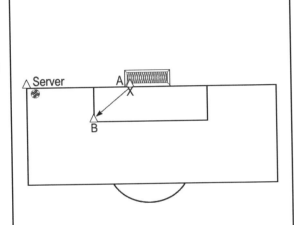

Organization:
The server throws the ball to the player, simulating a corner kick, who must jump to head it away. On landing the player must sprint to the cone to simulate moving forward to make a challenge or block a shot.

System of measurement:
Time the movement of the player from landing after the header to touching cone (B) with one foot.

Fitness Record

Date: Player Name:
Time from landing after the header to cone (B):

Date: Player Name:
Time from landing after the header to cone (B):

Date: Player Name:
Time from landing after the header to cone (B):

Date: Player Name:
Time from landing after the header to cone (B):

Date: Player Name:
Time from landing after the header to cone (B):

Date: Player Name:
Time from landing after the header to cone (B):

Date: Player Name:
Time from landing after the header to cone (B):

Date: Player Name:
Time from landing after the header to cone (B):

Training Variations:

This session can be performed as a rotation drill for fitness. Three players perform the drill and move clockwise to rotate between positions over a set time period. Have a player on cone (A), a player on cone (B) and a player as the server.

Set up layout on the other side of the goal and rotation can also be used around all 6 players.

Recover and start a new attack

Fitness Aims:
To train defensive players to recover to a defensive position and control the ball.
The player must to be able to run with the ball to the edge of the penalty area to start a new attack. The session should develop the speed, agility and timing of the defensive player.

Layout Description:
Use the penalty and goal areas for this session.
Set up a cone on each of the top corners of the goal area and the top corners of the penalty area and place the start cone (A) on the penalty spot.
Place two additional cones on the edge of the penalty area in line with the top of the goal area.

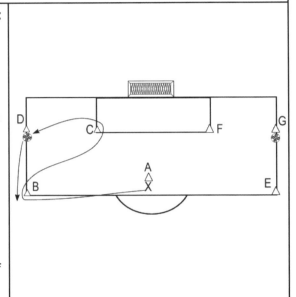

Organization:
The player starts with both heels touching cone (A) facing away from the goal. On the command 'GO' the player runs towards cone (B) and then around to cone (C) looking at the ball placed next to cone (D). After the player runs around cone C he should run to the ball, control it and run with it to the edge of the penalty area to pass the ball forward. The player then jogs back to cone (A) and repeats on the other side of the penalty area using cones (E), (F) and (G).

System of measurement:
Time the movement from the command 'GO' until the player makes contact with the ball with one foot.

Fitness Record

Date: Player Name:
Time from `GO` to contact the ball:

Date: Player Name:
Time from `GO` to contact the ball:

Date: Player Name:
Time from `GO` to contact the ball:

Date: Player Name:
Time from `GO` to contact the ball:

Date: Player Name:
Time from `GO` to contact the ball:

Date: Player Name:
Time from `GO` to contact the ball:

Date: Player Name:
Time from `GO` to contact the ball:

Training Variations:

The timing can include dribbling the ball to cone (B) or just let the player kick the ball away and time until first contact with the ball.

This can be trained with a group of players e.g. 5 or 6 where the recovery time is the number of players used. The player will start as soon as the last player finishes but this will require a number of balls to be placed at cone (D) and at cone (G).

Tracking back showing the inside

Fitness Aims:

To train defensive players in tracking back and showing their opponent the inside of the playing field.
The session should develop speed and coordination of the players.

Layout Description:

Place cone (A) 3 yards in from the sideline and level with the top edge of the penalty area. This is the start position.

Place cone (B) level with cone (A) and the top edge of the goal area.

Place cone (C) and a ball 1 yard from the cone on the corner of the goal area.

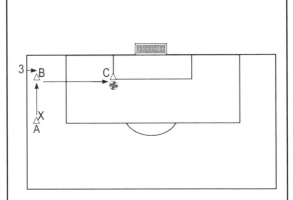

Organization:

The player starts with both heels touching cone (A) with his back to cone (B). On the command 'GO' the player runs backwards to cone (B) in a defensive stance showing the inside of the field until one foot touches cone (B), simulating tracking back. The player must then run across to cone (C) and strike the ball simulating making a clearance.

System of measurement:

Time the movement from the command 'GO' to the player striking the ball.

Fitness Record

Date: Player Name:
Time from `GO` to striking the ball:

Date: Player Name:
Time from `GO` to striking the ball:

Date: Player Name:
Time from `GO` to striking the ball:

Date: Player Name:
Time from `GO` to striking the ball:

Date: Player Name:
Time from `GO` to striking the ball:

Date: Player Name:
Time from `GO` to striking the ball:

Date: Player Name:
Time from `GO` to striking the ball:

Training Variations:

This session can be used as a rotation drill where 3 balls are placed at cone (C) and the player runs through the drill 3 times.

The time should be clocked from the command `GO` until the third ball is kicked as a clearance.
Place the 3 balls in such a manner that the drill can be reproduced i.e. 1 yard from the cone and 1 yard from each other.

Defending and showing the side line

Fitness Aims:

To train defensive players in tracking back to defend and show the opponent the sideline. The session should develop speed and coordination of the players.

Layout Description:	
Place cone (A) 3 yards in from the sideline and level with the edge of the penalty area. This is the start position. Place cone (B) and a ball level with cone (A) on the end line.	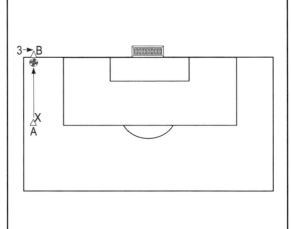

Organization:

The player starts with both heels touching cone (A) with his backs to cone (B). On the command 'GO' the player runs backwards to cone (B) in a defensive stance showing the outside of the field. On reaching cone (B) the player should strike the ball and kick it out of the playing field, simulating tracking back and making a last ditch tackle to prevent a cross.

System of measurement:

Time the movement from the command 'GO' to the player kicking the ball.

Fitness Record

Date: Player Name:
Time from `GO` to kicking the ball:

Date: Player Name:
Time from `GO` to kicking the ball:

Date: Player Name:
Time from `GO` to kicking the ball:

Date: Player Name:
Time from `GO` to kicking the ball:

Date: Player Name:
Time from `GO` to kicking the ball:

Date: Player Name:
Time from `GO` to kicking the ball:

Date: Player Name:
Time from `GO` to kicking the ball:

Training Variations:

This session can be set up as a series of 3 grids of cones (A and B) across the field. The layouts must be equal to the first (A and B) cones and 10 yards from each other. The player will then run from striking the ball to running diagonally to the start of the next set of cones.

Time the player from `GO`until striking the last ball.

Recovery to execute a tackle

Fitness Aims:

To train defensive players to recover and execute a tackle. The session should develop speed, agility, coordination and timing of the players.

Layout Description:

Layout 3 cones in a triangle.

Cone (A) 3 yards in from the sideline and level with the edge of the penalty area. Cone (B) 3 yards in from the sideline and level with edge of the goal area.

Cone (C) 10 yards in from the sideline and equal distance from cones (A) and (B). Place a ball 1 yard from cone(C).

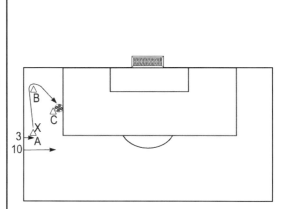

Organization:

The player starts with heels touching cone (A) and facing towards cone (B). On the command GO the player runs forward to cone (B) running outside the cone and touches it with one hand. The player must then run to cone (C) and strike the ball. This simulates recovery, keeping low to change direction and coordination to execute a tackle.

System of measurement:

Time the movement from the command 'GO' to the player striking the ball.

Fitness Record

Date: Player Name:
Time from `GO` to striking the ball:

Date: Player Name:
Time from `GO` to striking the ball:

Date: Player Name:
Time from `GO` to striking the ball:

Date: Player Name:
Time from `GO` to striking the ball:

Date: Player Name:
Time from `GO` to striking the ball:

Date: Player Name:
Time from `GO` to striking the ball:

Date: Player Name:
Time from `GO` to striking the ball:

Training Variations:

This session can be changed to running with the ball instead of just kicking the ball to the halfway line, simulating tackling and starting a new attack.
Time the play from `GO` until reaching the halfway line.

To make this into a drill rotate with 3 balls laid out on cone (C) 1 yard from each other and the player should run back to cone (A) to repeat the drill.
Time the player from `GO` until the last ball is kicked.

Recovery from the ground

Fitness Aims:

To train defensive players to get up and recover, control the ball and start a new attack.
This session should develop speed, agility and coordination of defensive players

Layout Description:	
Use the penalty and goal areas for this session Place cones on the top corners of both the goal and penalty areas and an additional cone on the penalty spot. Set up a cone on the top of the D for the server position.	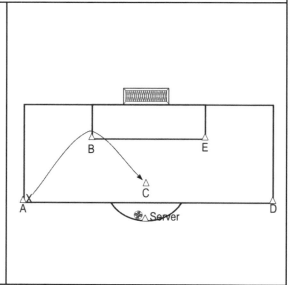

Organization:

The player starts lying down with both feet touching cone (A). On the command 'GO' the player gets up and sprints to and around cone (B) where the server will play the ball for the player to control quickly. The player then runs with the ball to cone (C) and plays it back to the server. Repeat the procedure on the other side of the goal with cones (D) and (E), ending up again with cone (C).

System of measurement:

Time the movement from the command 'GO' to the player touching cone (C) with one foot.

Fitness Record

Date: Player Name:
Time from `GO` to touching cone (C):

Date: Player Name:
Time from `GO` to touching cone (C):

Date: Player Name:
Time from `GO` to touching cone (C):

Date: Player Name:
Time from `GO` to touching cone (C):

Date: Player Name:
Time from `GO` to touching cone (C):

Date: Player Name:
Time from `GO` to touching cone (C):

Date: Player Name:
Time from `GO` to touching cone (C):

Training Variations:

Both sides should be timed individually (ABC) and (DEC).

This session can be used as a drill with 2 teams competing against each other. Use 2 severs and at least 3 players to a team. All players should be lying down and each team numbered e.g. from 1 to 3. On the command `GO` the server calls out a number and the player with that number should complete the drill. Teams should be changed over after all players have completed the drill on one side.

Diagonal recovery runs

Fitness Aims:

To train players in diagonal running when recovering to defend. This session will develop speed and agility.

Layout Description:	
Set up cone (A) on the corner of the penalty area. This is the start position. Set up cone (B) on the corner of the goal area.	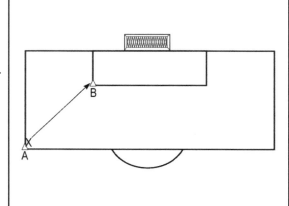

Organization:

The player starts with feet touching cone (A) facing away from cone (B). On the command `GO` the player must turn and sprint to cone (B) touching it with one foot.

System of measurement:

Time the movement from the command `GO` to player touching cone (B) with foot.

Fitness Record

Date: Defender's Name:
Time from `GO` to touching cone (B):

Date: Defender's Name:
Time from `GO` to touching cone (B):

Date: Defender's Name:
Time from `GO` to touching cone (B):

Date: Defender's Name:
Time from `GO` to touching cone (B):

Date: Defender's Name:
Time from `GO` to touching cone (B):

Date: Defender's Name:
Time from `GO` to touching cone (B):

Date: Defender's Name:
Time from `GO` to touching cone (B):

Training Variations:

The layout for this session could include cones placed on both intersections of the D, the middle of the goal area and the opposite corner of the goal area. This will mean that the player jogs to the next diagonal set of cones i.e. the intersection of the D to the middle of the six-yard area and repeats the diagonal run. Time all 3 runs separately.

By adding a cone on the opposite side of the penalty area the session can also be done in reverse.

Midfielder Fitness Training General

Functional Attributes:

Speed	Strength	Agility	Balance
Endurance	coordination	Timing	Rapid acceleration
Fast directional changes			

The Midfielder's Role:

The midfield players are the engine room of the team. They must be able to link the play between the attacking and defensive units.

These players must possess a range of qualities in order to carry out their individual and group role.

The midfielder player must possess speed and be able to make fast directional changes to close down an opponent and move into a supporting position.

They must have strength, balance and timing to make successful tackles and challenges against an opponent with the ball.

Agility is also needed to recover quickly from going to ground.

Wide midfield players may also be required to act as wing players and must have high endurance qualities in order to support attacking play and to recover quickly when ball possession is lost.

Midfielder Training Sessions:

These training sessions are specifically designed for midfield players and each exercise can be used as a test to evaluate the fitness progress by timing and recording a specific movement.

The exercises can also be used to train midfield players by combining several different sessions with different repetitions in a circuit.

Midfielder Fitness Training Sessions

1.   Running and changing direction
2.   The midfielder star run
3.   Recover run from a ground position
4.   Long pass, forward run and recovery
5.   Short recovery runs
6.   Recovering to defend
7.   Jump, land and run
8.   Recover and tackle
9.   Central recovery runs
10.   Running to support the attack

Equipment needed and the layout of the Training Sessions:

⊙   A set of cones for marking the training area.

⊙   A long tape measure for setting the distances for the training layout.

⊙   A stop watch for evaluating the fitness of the players.

⊙   At least one ball between two players.

⊙   First aid bag in case of injuries.

The sessions are laid out in and around the central area of the field to keep the perspective, whenever possible, on where the players would normally play.

Running and changing direction

Fitness Aims:
To train players in running and changing direction in the mid-field.
This session should develop speed and agility.

Layout Description:
Use the center area of the field for this drill.

Set out cone (A) on the sideline 10 yards from the halfway line.
This is the start position.

Set out cones (BCDE) around the center circle at the following positions
B - 6 o'clock, C - 9 o'clock
D - 3 o'clock, E -12 o'clock
Set up cone (F) on the opposite sideline to cone (A) and 10 yards from the halfway line.

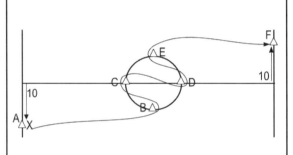

Organization:
The player starts with both feet behind and in contact with cone (A). On the command 'GO' the player runs to cone (B) then around outside of cones (CDE) ending up with cone (F). The player should run outside of each cone, keeping low on the turn and touching the cone with one hand.

System of measurement:
Time the movement from the command 'GO' to the player touching cone (F) with one hand.

Fitness Record

Date: Player Name:
Time from `GO` to touching cone (F):

Date: Player Name:
Time from `GO` to touching cone (F):

Date: Player Name:
Time from `GO` to touching cone (F):

Date: Player Name:
Time from `GO` to touching cone (F):

Date: Player Name:
Time from `GO` to touching cone (F):

Date: Player Name:
Time from `GO` to touching cone (F):

Date: Player Name:
Time from `GO` to touching cone (F):

Training Variations:

This drill can be used as a fitness session where players run after each other.
The player starts on cone (A) and as soon as the player reaches cone (B) the next player starts.
Wait for all players to finish and then the players run back in the opposite direction.

A ball can be used where the player dribbles around the cones to cone (F).

The midfielder star run

Fitness Aims:
To train players in running varied distances.
This session should develop speed, agility and coordination of the player.

Layout Description:	
Use in and around the center circle area for this drill. Set up a cone on the center spot. This is the start cone and start position. Set up cones at 5,10,15, 20,25 yards from the center start cone set out in a random pattern.	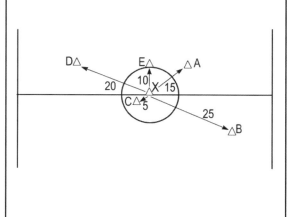

Organization:
The player starts with both feet in contact with the start cone facing forwards. On the command 'GO' the player runs clockwise around the 'Star' by running to a cone and touching it with one foot then returning to the start cone after each distance.
The player must complete all 5 runs, but may start at any point in the star although he must move clockwise and cover all distances.

System of measurement:
Record the number of completed runs in 1 minute or time taken to cover one completed run.
A complete run = from the start cone to each cone on the star and back to the start cone covering all distances.

Fitness Record

Date: Player Name:
Number of completed runs in 1 minute:

Date: Player Name:
Number of completed runs in 1 minute:

Date: Player Name:
Number of completed runs in 1 minute:

Date: Player Name:
Number of completed runs in 1 minute:

Date: Player Name:
Number of completed runs in 1 minute:

Date: Player Name:
Number of completed runs in 1 minute:

Date: Player Name:
Number of completed runs in 1 minute:

Training Variations:

This drill can be used with 2 to 3 players chasing each other when used specifically as a fitness activity .

The players start around the start cone and at different points in the star and all players must run around the star in the same direction.

Match players in fitness and performance in order to encourage competition.

Recovery run from a ground position

Fitness Aims:
To train players to make a recovery run after performing a tackle and going to ground.
This session should develop agility, strength and the endurance qualities of the player.

Layout Description:
Set up this drill 10 yards either side of the half way line.

Set up a channel over a distance of 20 yards with cones set out at 3 yards apart to form two gates (A and B).

Gate (A) is the start position.

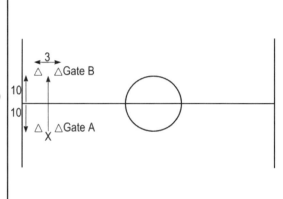

Organization:
The player adopts a prone position to simulate making a tackle and falling on the ground. The body must be behind the line of gate (A). On the command 'GO' the player gets up and runs to gate (B) and adopts a lying position. The player must recover and get up and run back to gate (A) and repeat the same action.

System of measurement:
Time the movement from the command 'GO' for 1 minute and record the number of completed legs performed in the time limit (complete leg = A to B or B to A).

Fitness Record

Date: Player Name:
Number of completed runs in 1 minute:

Date: Player Name:
Number of completed runs in 1 minute:

Date: Player Name:
Number of completed runs in 1 minute:

Date: Player Name:
Number of completed runs in 1 minute:

Date: Player Name:
Number of completed runs in 1 minute:

Date: Player Name:
Number of completed runs in 1 minute:

Date: Player Name:
Number of completed runs in 1 minute:

Training Variations:

For fitness drills set up 2 channels and have 2 players race against each over a specific time.

For a team fitness drill have 5 players behind gate (A) lying down and 1 player at a time gets up and runs to the other gate. When the fifth player arrives at gate (A) they touch the hand of the next player who repeats the process to gate (B).

Long pass, forward run and recovery

Fitness Aims:
To train players to make supporting runs after executing a long forward pass and recover to a defensive position.
This session should develop speed and coordination of the player.

Layout Description:
Set out cone (A) on the edge of the penalty area. This is the start position.
Set up cones (BCD) on the half way line 10 yards apart.
Set up 2 target boxes on the corners of the other penalty area.

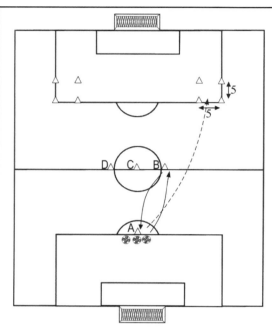

Organization:
On the command `GO` the player must collect a ball from cone (A) and execute a long forward pass to either target box.
The player must then run forward to one of the designated cones to simulate a supporting run to support the play and then recover to cone (A).

System of measurement:
Time the movement for one completed run (Complete run = A to B or A to C or A to D).

Fitness Record

Date: Player Name:
Time for a complete run:

Date: Player Name:
Time for a complete run:

Date: Player Name:
Time for a complete run:

Date: Player Name:
Time for a complete run:

Date: Player Name:
Time for a complete run:

Date: Player Name:
Time for a complete run:

Date: Player Name:
Time for a complete run:

Training Variations:

The player can collect a ball from cone (A) and dribble it to cone (B) and execute a long forward pass to either target box. The player then collects the next ball and dribbles to cone (C) and executes the long pass and repeats a long pass with the last ball after dribbling to cone (D).

Time from the command `GO` until returning to the start cone (A) after executing the third and last long forward pass.

Short recovery runs

Fitness Aims:
To train players to make short recovery runs.
This session should develop speed and agility of the player.

Layout Description:
Set up cone (A) on the intersection of the sideline and halfway line. This is the start position.

Set up cones (BCDEFG) across the pitch towards the opposite sideline. Cone (B) must be diagonal to cone (A) and 10 yards away and in line with the top of the center circle.
Cones (CDE) should be at 9,12,3 o'clock respectively around center circle. Cones (F) and (G) are a mirror of cones (B) and (A).

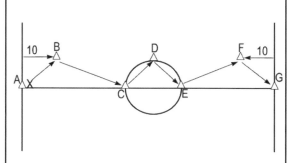

Organization:
The player starts with both feet behind and in contact with cone (A). On the command 'GO' the player runs forward to cone (B) touching it with one hand and keeping low to change direction. The player then runs to cones (CDEFG), touching each cone with the hand and finishes at cone (G).

System of measurement:
Time the movement for one completed run form cone (A) to cone (G).

Fitness Record

Date: Player Name:
Time from the command `GO` to cone (G):

Date: Player Name:
Time from the command `GO` to cone (G):

Date: Player Name:
Time from the command `GO` to cone (G):

Date: Player Name:
Time from the command `GO` to cone (G):

Date: Player Name:
Time from the command `GO` to cone (G):

Date: Player Name:
Time from the command `GO` to cone (G):

Date: Player Name:
Time from the command `GO` to cone (G):

Training Variations:

This drill can be used as a fitness session where all players run after each other.
The player starts on cone (A) and as soon as the player reaches cone (B) the next player starts.
Wait for all players to finish and then the players run in the opposite direction.

This drill can include a ball where the players dribble around each cone still touching the cone with one hand.

Recovering to defend

Fitness Aims:
To train players in making long recovery runs when possession is lost after supporting the attack.
This drill should develop speed and agility.

Layout Description:	
Set up cones to form gate (A) on the side and corner of the penalty area. Set up cones to form gate (B) on the same side and cor-ner of the opposite penalty area. Player start position is inside the center circle.	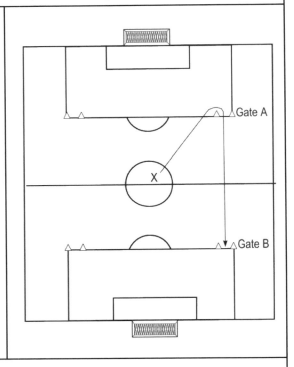

Organization:
The player must start inside the center circle and jog to gate (A). The player must then turn and run from gate (A) to gate (B) as quickly as possible.
This simulates recovering to defend when possession is lost and is a penalty area to penalty area run.

System of measurement:
Time the movement of player passing through gate (A) to player passing through gate (B).

Fitness Record

Date: Player Name:
Time from gate (A) to gate (B):

Date: Player Name:
Time from gate (A) to gate (B):

Date: Player Name:
Time from gate (A) to gate (B):

Date: Player Name:
Time from gate (A) to gate (B):

Date: Player Name:
Time from gate (A) to gate (B):

Date: Player Name:
Time from gate (A) to gate (B):

Date: Player Name:
Time from gate (A) to gate (B):

Training Variations:

This session can be a repetition drill where the player jogs back to the center circle from gate (B) and repeats the drill 5 times. Check each time and average out the times to get a true value of fitness.

Set up 2 more gates on the opposite side of the field and have 2 players running at the same time.

As a team training drill put all players in the center circle. The first player jogs to gate (A) and when they arrive at gate (A) the next player starts while the first player sprints to gate (B). Have all players jog back to the center circle.

Jump, land and run

Fitness Aims:

To train players in jumping, landing and running.
The session should develop speed, agility and muscular
strength of players.

Layout Description:

Set up cone (A) in
the center spot and
cones (B and C) in a
triangle with cone
(A) 10 yards apart
around the center
circle.

This would be the
area in which the
player being trained
would normally oper-
ate in a game.

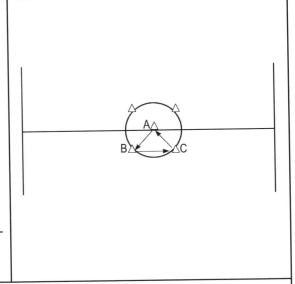

Organization:

The player starts with both heels touching cone (A). On the
command 'GO' the player jumps vertically taking off with 1 foot.
The player must land on both feet and run to cone (B) and
repeat the same jump and landing and then run on to cone (C).
The player must touch each cone before jumping.

System of measurement:

Record the number of Jumps - Landings - Runs in 1 minute.

Fitness Record

Date: Player Name:
Number of jumps and landings in 1 minute:

Date: Player Name:
Number of jumps and landings in 1 minute:

Date: Player Name:
Number of jumps and landings in 1 minute:

Date: Player Name:
Number of jumps and landings in 1 minute:

Date: Player Name:
Number of jumps and landings in 1 minute:

Date: Player Name:
Number of jumps and landings in 1 minute:

Date: Player Name:
Number of jumps and landings in 1 minute:

Training Variations:

Place 2 more cones on the opposite side to cones (B and C) on the center circle. Have a player on cones (B, C, D and E) and on the command `GO` the players jump and run to cone (A) and on to the next cone clockwise.
Time from the command `GO` until the last player reaches the starting cone after 1 round clockwise.
Then time from the command `GO` until the last player reaches the starting cone after 1 round counter-clockwise.

Recover and tackle

Fitness Aims:

To train players in making recovery runs and side tackles. The session should develop speed, agility and coordination of the players.

Layout Description:	
Set up cone (A) on the corner of the penalty area. Set cone (B) on the corner of the goal area. Set up cone (C) on the penalty area and level with cone (B). Place a ball on the sideline and 1 yard from cone (C).	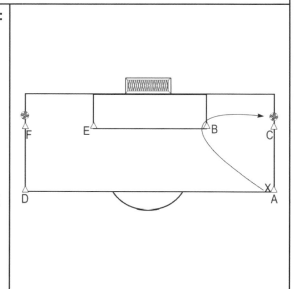

Organization:

The player starts with 1 foot touching cone (A). On the command 'GO' the player runs around cone (B) touching it with 1 hand and then runs on to cone (C) to execute a tackle with a stationary ball.

System of measurement:

Time the movement from the command 'GO' to the player making contact with the ball.

Fitness Record
Date:　　　　Player Name: Time from the command `GO` to the player making contact with the ball:
Date:　　　　Player Name: Time from the command `GO` to the player making contact with the ball:
Date:　　　　Player Name: Time from the command `GO` to the player making contact with the ball:
Date:　　　　Player Name: Time from the command `GO` to the player making contact with the ball:
Date:　　　　Player Name: Time from the command `GO` to the player making contact with the ball:
Date:　　　　Player Name: Time from the command `GO` to the player making contact with the ball:

Training Variations:

Set cones up the same way but on both sides of the penalty area.

Have 2 players run at the same time and check who reaches the ball first.

The players must run the drill on both sides of the penalty area.

Central recovery runs

Fitness Aims:

To train players to make central recovery runs.
The session should improve speed and agility.

Layout Description:

Place cone (A) on the center spot.

Set up cones (BCDE) 15 yards from the center line.

The cones (BE) and (CD) should be 30 yards from each other and 5 yards from either side of the center circle.

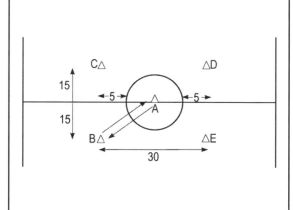

Organization:

The player starts with 1 foot touching the start cone A. On the command 'GO' the player runs forward to cone B and then backward to cone (A). Repeat for cones (C, D and E). The player must touch the cones with 1 foot each time before returning to cone (A).

System of measurement:

Time from the command 'GO' to the player making a complete run through cones: (A) to (B) to (A) - (A) to (C) to (A) - (A) to (D) to (A) -- (A) to (E) to (A).

Fitness Record

Date: Player Name:
Time from cone (A) until reaching cone (A) after the run to cone (E):

Date: Player Name:
Time from cone (A) until reaching cone (A) after the run to cone (E):

Date: Player Name:
Time from cone (A) until reaching cone (A) after the run to cone (E):

Date: Player Name:
Time from cone (A) until reaching cone (A) after the run to cone (E):

Date: Player Name:
Time from cone (A) until reaching cone (A) after the run to cone (E):

Training Variations:

For longer runs the player should start on cone (A) run to cone (B) and then directly to cone (D), not stopping at cone (A), and back to cone (A). This should be repeated for cone (C) and cone (E).

This drill can be used with 4 players when used specifically as a fitness activity.
The players start around the start cone and run to a specific cone.
All players must run around the cones in the same direction.

Running to support the attack

Fitness Aims:

To train players in supporting runs with recovery.
The session should develop speed.

Layout Description:

Use the whole field and set out cones on the corners of the penalty areas and on the penalty spots. Create two gates on the center circle with cones placed on the intersection of the center circle and the half way line. Place another cone outside these cones at 2 yards apart, to create a gate.

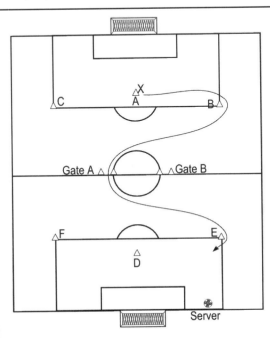

Organization:

The player starts with one foot touching cone (A).
On the command 'GO' the player runs around cone (B), through gate (A) and around cone (E) where a ball is passed to the player who must control and shoot the ball into the goal.

System of measurement:

Time the movement from the command 'GO' to the player reaching cone (E) and the first contact with the ball. The time on the ball does not count.

Fitness Record

Date: Player Name:
Time from the command `GO` to the players contact with the ball:

Date: Player Name:
Time from the command `GO` to the players contact with the ball:

Date: Player Name:
Time from the command `GO` to the players contact with the ball:

Date: Player Name:
Time from the command `GO` to the players contact with the ball:

Date: Player Name:
Time from the command `GO` to the players contact with the ball:

Date: Player Name:
Time from the command `GO` to the players contact with the ball:

Training Variations:

After the first run from cone (A) to cone (E) the player should jog back to cone (A) and repeat the run on the opposite side of the field, running first around cone C, through gate B and ending at cone F.
Time both runs and check the difference in time.

The session can be used where 2 players can run at the same time, 1 from cone (A) and the other from cone D and in opposite directions to each other.

Attacker Fitness Training General

Functional Attributes:

Speed	Strength	Agility	Rapid acceleration
Coordination	Timing	Balance	and deceleration

The Attacker's Role:

The attacking player is the spearhead of the team, and the first line of defense which means that he must work hard to put the opposing teams' defensive unit under pressure when possession is lost.

This requires endurance coupled with speed and fast directional changes to either create attacking opportunities or to recover and close down opposing defenders in possession of the ball.

The attacker needs good timing, balance and coordination to create good goal scoring opportunities, and must be prepared to take the opportunity to capitalize on the opposing defense making mistakes.

This may entail getting up quickly from the ground and reacting to a loose ball opportunity.

Attacker Training Sessions:

These training sessions are specifically designed for use by attacking players and each exercise can be used as a test to evaluate the fitness progress by timing and recording a singular movement.

The exercises can also be used to train attackers by using several different sessions with different repetitions in a circuit.

Attacker Fitness Training Sessions

1.   Recover and defend
2.   Finishing from crosses
3.   Change of direction and pace
4.   Recover off the ground
5.   Running beyond the defense
6.   The strikers star run
7.   The spin off and change of direction
8.   Attacking runs
9.   Diagonal runs and changing direction
10. Run to strike the ball

Equipment needed and the layout of the Training Sessions:

⊛   A set of cones for marking the training area.

⊛   A long tape measure for setting the distances for the training layout.

⊛   A stop watch for evaluating the fitness of the players.

⊛   At least one ball between two players.

⊛   First aid bag in case of injuries.

The sessions are laid out in and around the penalty area to keep the perspective on where the players would normally play whenever possible.

Recover and defend

Fitness Aims:

To train attacking players to recover and defend.
This session should develop speed, agility and balance.

Layout Description: Use the penalty and goal areas for this session. Place cones at the corners of the goal and the penalty areas. Place 2 additional cones on the inter-sections of the D with the penalty area and 1 on the penalty spot.	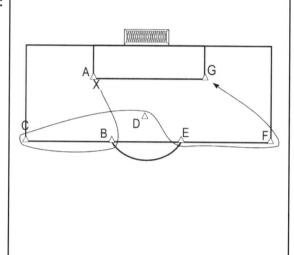

Organization:

The player starts with both heels in contact with start cone (A).
On the command 'GO' the player runs around cones (B, C, D, E, F) and ends up at cone (G). The player should run outside each cone, touching them with 1 hand and end up touching cone (G) with a foot. This session can be repeated in the opposite direction starting with cone (G) and ending at cone (A).

System of measurement:

Time the player from the command 'GO' to the player touching cone (G) with one foot.

Fitness Record

Date: Player Name:
Time from the command `GO` to touching cone (G) with one foot:

Date: Player Name:
Time from the command `GO` to touching cone (G) with one foot:

Date: Player Name:
Time from the command `GO` to touching cone (G) with one foot:

Date: Player Name:
Time from the command `GO` to touching cone (G) with one foot:

Date: Player Name:
Time from the command `GO` to touching cone (G) with one foot:

Training Variations:

Instead of touching cone (G) with the foot place a ball on the corner of the goal area.

This drill can be done with a defensive player defending against the attacker. The defender must protect the goal at all times and prevent the attacker from going to the ball from cone (F) to cone (G) without creating a foul.

When used specifically as a fitness activity have 4 players running after each other. The next player should start when the previous reaches cone (D). Place 4 balls on the goal area and each player should shoot the ball at the end.

Finishing from crosses

Fitness Aims:
To train attacking players in running towards the ball, from a cross, and getting in front of defenders and attacking the ball. The session should develop speed and the ability to get to the ball first.

Layout Description:
Use the penalty and goal areas for this session.
Place cones in line with the penalty spot, one on each side of the penalty area, each one in line with the goal area and one on the penalty spot itself. Place 2 more cones on the top of the penalty area in line with the goal area and the start cone at the top of the D.

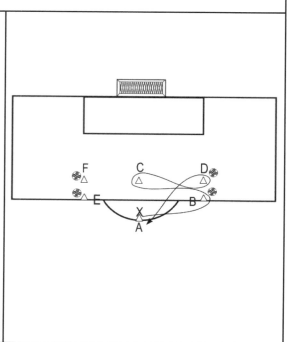

Organization:
The player starts with both heels touching cone (A) facing away from the goal. On the command 'GO' the player runs to cone (B), controls the ball and shoots it into the goal. The player then runs around cone (B) and then around cone (C) to come and collect another ball at cone (D) to shoot into the goal. The player then runs around cone (D) finishing at cone (A). The player should repeat the procedure running towards cone (E) around cone (C) to cone (F).

System of measurement:
Time the movement from the command 'GO' to the player making a complete run from cone (A) shooting all four balls and ending at the start cone (A).

Fitness Record

Date: Player Name:
Time from the command `GO` to touching cone (A) after shooting all 4 balls:

Date: Player Name:
Time from the command `GO` to touching cone (A) after shooting all 4 balls:

Date: Player Name:
Time from the command `GO` to touching cone (A) after shooting all 4 balls:

Date: Player Name:
Time from the command `GO` to touching cone (A) after shooting all 4 balls:

Date: Player Name:
Time from the command `GO` to touching cone (A) after shooting all 4 balls:

Date: Player Name:
Time from the command `GO` to touching cone (A) after shooting all 4 balls:

Training Variations:

Players acting as defenders can occupy both cones (B and D). The defender must keep one foot on the cone but can disrupt the attacking player.

The balls must be placed out of reach of the defenders but close enough to be a distraction to the attacker.

The attacking player must keep watching the ball while he runs around the cones.

Change of direction and pace

Fitness Aims:
To train attacking players to change direction and pace.
This session should develop speed and agility.
Player must make directional changes.

Layout Description:
Use the penalty and goal areas for this session.

Place cones on each corner of the goal area and 1 on the penalty spot.

Place 2 additional cones on the inter-sections of the D with the penalty area.

Place the start cone (A) 10 yards from the top of the D, inline with the penal-ty spot.

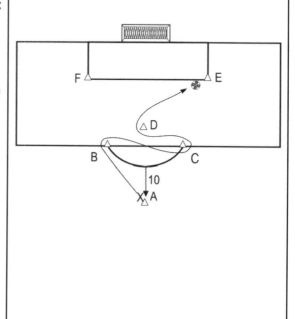

Organization:
The player starts with both feet heels in contact with the start cone (A) facing the goal. On the command 'GO' the player sprints to cone (B). The player then changes pace and direction and jogs from cone (B) around cone (C) to cone (D). The player ends up sprinting from cone (D) to cone (E), shooting the ball into the goal.
By using cone (C) as the first cone to run to, the player would end up shooting a ball at cone (F).

System of measurement:
Time movement of the player from the command 'GO' to the player reaching cone (B) and the time from cone (D) to striking the ball.

Fitness Record

Date: Player Name:
Time from the command `GO` to cone (B):
Time from cone (D) to striking the ball:

Date: Player Name:
Time from the command `GO` to cone (B):
Time from cone (D) to striking the ball:

Date: Player Name:
Time from the command `GO` to cone (B):
Time from cone (D) to striking the ball:

Date: Player Name:
Time from the command `GO` to cone (B):
Time from cone (D) to striking the ball:

Date: Player Name:
Time from the command `GO` to cone (B):
Time from cone (D) to striking the ball:

Training Variations:

Add an additional ball at cone (F) and the player can shoot the ball at cone (E) and then run around cone (E) to shoot the ball at cone (F).

Have a player acting as a defender who starts on cone (A) with the attacker. The defender should follow the attacker around the cones until cone (D), where he should run inside protecting the goal and prevent the attacker from scoring without fouling.

Recover off the ground

Fitness Aims:

To train attacking players to get up quickly from the ground and recover to a specific point and execute a first time shot on goal. This session should develop speed and agility.

Layout Description:	
Use the penalty and goal areas for this session Place cones on each corner of the goal area and one on the penalty spot.	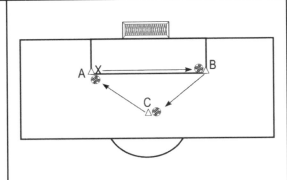

Organization:

The player starts at cone (A) lying on the ground with the feet touching the cone. On the command 'GO' the player gets up and runs to cone (B) and shoots the ball into the goal. The player then adopts a lying position with the feet touching cone (B) and immediately gets up and repeats the same procedure by running to cone (C). At cone (C) the procedure is repeated to end up at cone (A), shooting the third ball into the goal.

System of measurement:

Record the number of completed runs in 1 minute (complete run = cone (A) to cone (B), cone (B) to cone (C), cone (C) to cone (A)).
Player must adopt a lying position at each cone before continuing.

Fitness Record

Date: Player Name:
Number of complete runs in 1 minute:

Date: Player Name:
Number of complete runs in 1 minute:

Date: Player Name:
Number of complete runs in 1 minute:

Date: Player Name:
Number of complete runs in 1 minute:

Date: Player Name:
Number of complete runs in 1 minute:

Date: Player Name:
Number of complete runs in 1 minute:

Date: Player Name:
Number of complete runs in 1 minute:

Training Variations:

Change the procedure where the ball is shot after getting up from the ground instead of before they adopt a lying position.

This time do not use a ball and have a player on each cone. The players should pursue each other trying to overtake. If a player is overtaken he drops out. Keep the time restricted to 30 seconds or maximum 1 minute but make sure all players adopt a proper lying position at each cone.

Running beyond the defense

Fitness Aims:

To train attacking players to run beyond and behind the defense and create space in the penalty area.
This session should develop speed and endurance.

Layout Description:

Set up the start cone on the center spot.

Set up cones to create 3-yard gate (A) on the outside of the center circle.

Set up cones to create a 3-yard gate (B) with 1 cone set on the intersection with the D on the edge of the penalty area. Gate (B) can be either side of the D.

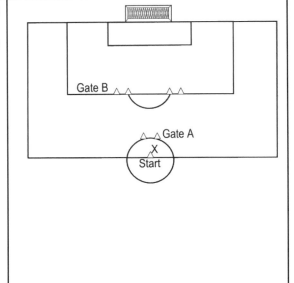

Organization:

On the command 'GO' the player jogs from the start cone to gate (A). At gate (A) the player must then sprint to gate (B) to simulate running beyond the defense at an angle.

System of measurement:

Record time of movement from gate (A) to gate (B).

Fitness Record

Date: Player Name:
Time from gate (A) to gate (B):

Date: Player Name:
Time from gate (A) to gate (B):

Date: Player Name:
Time from gate (A) to gate (B):

Date: Player Name:
Time from gate (A) to gate (B):

Date: Player Name:
Time from gate (A) to gate (B):

Date: Player Name:
Time from gate (A) to gate (B):

Date: Player Name:
Time from gate (A) to gate (B):

Training Variations:

Have the player collect a ball at gate (A) and run with the ball to gate (B). Time the player from gate (A) to running through gate (B).

Vary the position of the gates so that the player runs to the corners of the penalty area. Play a ball from the center spot at the same time the player starts running to gate (B), where the player should run, control the ball and shoot on goal.

Vary the distance from gate (A) to gate (B) depending on the player's age and fitness.

The striker's 'star run'

Fitness Aims:
To train attacking players in running varied distances.
This session should develop speed, agility and coordination.

Layout Description:
Use the penalty and goal areas for this session.
Place a cone on the corner of the goal area and one on the corner of the penalty area.
Place another cone on the opposite side of the penalty area in line with the top of the goal area.
Place two additional cones on the intersections of the D with the penalty area and the starting cone directly on the penalty spot.

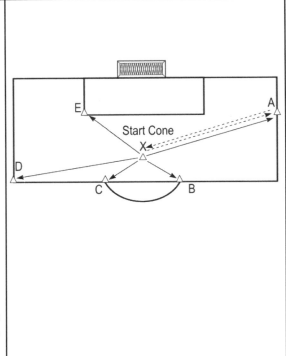

Organization:
The player starts with both feet in contact with the start cone (A) facing the field. On the command 'GO' the player runs in one direction around the 'Star', touching each cone with 1 foot and returning to the start cone each time. The player must complete all 5 runs. Although he may start at any point in the star, he must move around in one direction.

System of measurement:
Record the number of completed runs in 1 minute
A completed run = Start cone to each cone on the star and back to the start cone.

Fitness Record

Date: Player Name:
Number of completed runs in 1 minute:

Date: Player Name:
Number of completed runs in 1 minute:

Date: Player Name:
Number of completed runs in 1 minute:

Date: Player Name:
Number of completed runs in 1 minute:

Date: Player Name:
Number of completed runs in 1 minute:

Date: Player Name:
Number of completed runs in 1 minute:

Date: Player Name:
Number of completed runs in 1 minute:

Training Variations:

This drill can be used with 2 or 3 players when used specifically as a fitness activity. The players stand around the start cone facing different points in the star. The players select which is their starting cone in the star. All players must run around the star in the same direction.

If a player overtakes another player then the overtaken player drops out. Keep the time to a maximum of 1 minute.

The spin off and change direction

Fitness Aims:

To train attacking players to spin off and turn around a defender.
This session should develop speed and agility.

Layout Description:

Use the penalty and
the goal areas for
this session.

Place cones on each
corner of the goal
area and one on the
penalty spot.

Place 2 additional
cones on the inter-
sections of the D
with the penalty
area.

Place a ball at cone
(E).

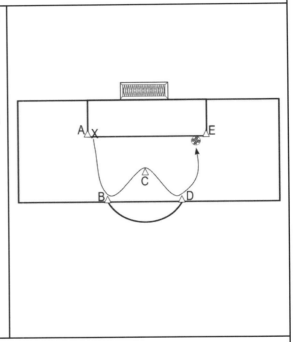

Organization:
The player starts with both heels touching cone (A) facing away
from the goal. On the command 'GO' the player runs to cone
(B), touches the cone with a foot, then makes a spin off move
and runs diagonally around cone (C) and then to cone (D).
When the player reaches cone (D) he should make a spin off
move and sprint to cone (E), shooting the ball into the goal.
This session can be repeated in the opposite direction starting
with cone (E) and a ball at cone (A).

System of measurement:
Time the movement from the command 'GO' to the player
shooting the ball into the goal.

Fitness Record

Date: Player Name:
Time from the command `GO` to shooting the ball:

Date: Player Name:
Time from the command `GO` to shooting the ball:

Date: Player Name:
Time from the command `GO` to shooting the ball:

Date: Player Name:
Time from the command `GO` to shooting the ball:

Date: Player Name:
Time from the command `GO` to shooting the ball:

Date: Player Name:
Time from the command `GO` to shooting the ball:

Date: Player Name:
Time from the command `GO` to shooting the ball:

Training Variations:

An extra ball can be added at cone (C) and the player should shoot the ball and continue the run.

Players acting as defenders can occupy cones (B and D). The defender must keep 1 foot touching the cone and the attacking player must run around the defender and spin off.

Attacking runs

Fitness Aims:

To train attacking players in making attacking runs.
This session should develop speed and agility.

Layout Description:	
Use the penalty and goal areas for this session. Place cones on each corner of the goal area and the penalty area. Place two additional cones on the intersections of the D with the penalty area and one at the top of the D. Place a ball at 1 yard from both cones (D and G).	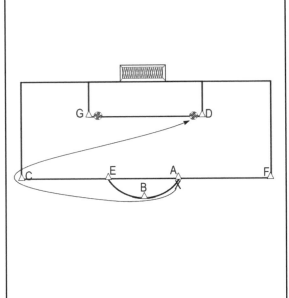

Organization:

The player starts with 1 foot touching cone (A). On the command 'GO' the player runs diagonally around cone (B) to (C) and then makes a diagonal run across the penalty area towards cone (D). The player shoots the ball at cone (D). Alternatively, start by using cone (E) as the start cone and shoot the ball at cone (G) using the other foot.

System of measurement:

Time the movement from the command 'GO' to the player striking the ball.

Fitness Record

Date: Player Name:
Time from the command `GO` to striking the ball at
1. Cone (D):
2. Cone (G):

Date: Player Name:
Time from the command `GO` to striking the ball at
1. Cone (D):
2. Cone (G):

Date: Player Name:
Time from the command `GO` to striking the ball at
1. Cone (D):
2. Cone (G):

Date: Player Name:
Time from the command `GO` to striking the ball at
1. Cone (D):
2. Cone (G):

Date: Player Name:
Time from the command `GO` to striking the ball at
1. Cone (D):
2. Cone (G):

Training Variations:

Players acting as defenders can occupy cones (D and G). The defender must keep 1 foot touching the cone but can disrupt the attacking player's shot.

Place the ball out of range of the defender but close enough to be a distraction to the attacker.

Diagonal runs and changing direction

Fitness Aims:

To train attacking players to make diagonal runs and change direction.
This session should develop speed and agility.

Layout Description:

Use the penalty and goal areas for this session.

Place cones at the corners of the goal area and the penalty area.

Place two additional cones on the inter-sections of the D with the penalty area and one on the penalty spot.

Set the last cone on the top of the D in line with the penalty spot.

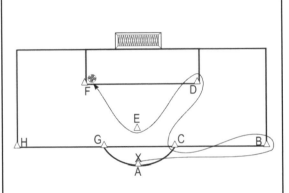

Organization:
The player starts with 1 foot touching cone (A). On the command 'GO' the player runs around the outside of each cone (B C D) and (E) ending at cone (F), shooting the ball into the goal. Practice both directions e.g. cones (A to H G F) and (E) ending at cone (D) shooting the ball.

System of measurement:
Time the movement from the command 'GO' to the player making a complete run from cone (A) through cones (B, C, D) and (E) to the player striking the ball.

Fitness Record

Date: Player Name:
Time from the command `GO` to shooting the ball:

Date: Player Name:
Time from the command `GO` to shooting the ball:

Date: Player Name:
Time from the command `GO` to shooting the ball:

Date: Player Name:
Time from the command `GO` to shooting the ball:

Date: Player Name:
Time from the command `GO` to shooting the ball:

Date: Player Name:
Time from the command `GO` to shooting the ball:

Date: Player Name:
Time from the command `GO` to shooting the ball:

Training Variations:

Players acting as defenders can occupy cones (D and F). The defender must keep 1 foot touching the cone but the defender on cone (F) can disrupt the attacking player's shot.

Place 5 balls on the goal area line at cone (F) and have 5 players run through the cones shooting 1 ball each. As soon as the player reaches cone (B), the next player can start the run.

Use both directions so that the players must shoot once with the left foot and once with the right foot.

Run to strike the ball

Fitness Aims:
To train attacking players to run and strike the ball.
This session should develop speed, timing and coordination.

Layout Description:	
Use the penalty and goal areas for this session. Set out cones on the outside line of the penalty area with one opposite the penalty spot and one each in line with the goal area. Place 2 more cones on the corners of the penalty area. Set the start cone on the top of the D in line with the penalty spot 10 yards from the top of the penal-ty area. Place a ball at each cone.	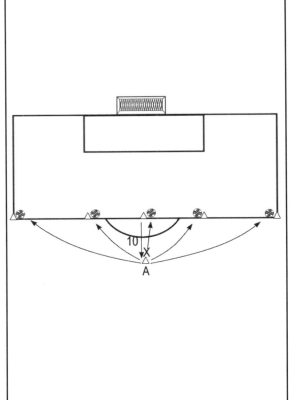

Organization:
The player starts with 1 foot touching cone (A). On the com-mand 'GO' the player runs and shoots each of the 5 balls into the goal in any sequence. The player must return to cone (A) after shooting each ball. Accuracy is important but the empha-sis must be on speed of movement and not on goals scored. Encourage the player to use the left foot for balls on the left side and right foot for balls on the right side.

System of measurement:
Time the movement from the command 'GO' to the player returning to cone (A) after striking the last ball.

Fitness Record

Date: Player Name:
Time from the command `GO` to touching cone (A) after shooting all 5 balls:

Date: Player Name:
Time from the command `GO` to touching cone (A) after shooting all 5 balls:

Date: Player Name:
Time from the command `GO` to touching cone (A) after shooting all 5 balls:

Date: Player Name:
Time from the command `GO` to touching cone (A) after shooting all 5 balls:

Date: Player Name:
Time from the command `GO` to touching cone (A) after shooting all 5 balls:

Date: Player Name:
Time from the command `GO` to touching cone (A) after shooting all 5 balls:

Training Variations:

Set out 10 balls, 2 on each cone and have 2 players alternate at running to take the shot. The first player runs to shoot the ball and returns to touch the hand of the second player who runs to shoot the next ball. This can be alternated between cones or the same cone each time.

Players acting as defenders can occupy the cones. The defender must keep 1 foot touching the cone but can distract the attacking player.

Also Available from Reedswain

#185 **Conditioning for Soccer** ————
by Raymond Verheijen
$19.95

#188 **300 Innovative Soccer Drills** ————————
by Roger Wilkinson and Mick Critchell
$14.95

#290 **Practice Plans for Effective
     Training** ————————————
by Ken Sherry
$14.95

#787 **Attacking Schemes and
     Training Exercises** ————————————
by Eugenio Fascetti and Romedio Scaia
$14.95

#788 **Zone Play** ————————
by Angelo Pereni and Michele di Cesare
$14.95

#792 **120 Competitive Games and
     Exercises** ————————————
by Nicola Pica
$14.95

#793 **Coaching the 5-3-2** ————————
by Eugenio Fascetti and Romedio Scaia
$14.95

www.reedswain.com or 800-331-5191

Also Available from Reedswain

#149 Soccer Tactics ————————
by Massimo Lucchesi
$12.95

#243 Coaching Team Shape ————————
by Emilio Cecchini
$12.95

#249 Coaching the 3-4-3 ————————
by Massimo Lucchesi
$12.95

#256 The Creative Dribbler ————————
by Peter Schreiner
$14.95

#265 Coordination, Agility and Speed Training for Soccer ————————
by Peter Schreiner
$14.95

#794 248 Drills for Attacking Soccer ————————
by Alessandro del Freo
$14.95

#905 Soccer Strategies ————————
by Robyn Jones and Tom Tranter
$12.95

www.reedswain.com or 800-331-5191